12/11/2018

D1153916

SCREENING TRAFFICKING

SCREENING TRAFFICKING

Prudent and Perilous

Yana Hashamova

Central European University Press
Budapest–New York

© 2018 by Yana Hashamova

Published in 2018 by

Central European University Press

Nádor utca 11, H-1051 Budapest, Hungary
Tel: +36-1-327-3138 or 327-3000
Fax: +36-1-327-3183
E-mail: ceupress@press.ceu.edu
Website: www.ceupress.com

224 West 57th Street, New York NY 10019, USA

All rights reserved. No part of this publication may be reproduced,
stored in a retrieval system, or transmitted, in any form or by any means,
without the permission of the Publisher.

The Library of Congress has cataloged this record under
LCCN: 2018000793

Printed in Hungary by
Prime Rate Kft., Budapest

To Lorenzo, for his unfailing
curiosity and brightness!

Table of Contents

PART ONE: THE VIEWER

PART TWO: THE REPRESENTATION

Lists of Tables and Plates

LIST OF TABLES

LIST OF FIGURES

LIST OF PLATES

CHAPTER 2:

CHAPTER 6

Acknowledgements

I became interested in the topic of human trafficking a decade ago, and since then I have organized conferences, delivered presentations, and advanced my research both through fieldwork with non-governmental organizations (NGOs) and through film and media investigations. In the meantime, numerous other projects and commitments interfered and sidetracked this monograph, but I was determined to finish it. I am particularly grateful for the financial support from IREX, the Mershon Center for International Security Studies, the Coca-Cola Critical Difference for Women Grant, and the Arts and Humanities Division of the Arts and Sciences College at the Ohio State University (OSU). Their funding aided my numerous visits to Balkan NGOs over the years.

Several NGOs have been extremely helpful, allowing me to examine their archives and reports and patiently responding to my inquiries. I am deeply indebted first and foremost to the leaders of *Asotsiatsiia Animus/Animus Association Foundation* (Sofia, Bulgaria), who connected me to other NGOs and who repeatedly accommodated my visits over the years. Other organizations which assisted me include *Otvorena Porta/Open Gate* (Skopje, Macedonia), *Otvori ochi/Open Your Eyes* (Resen, Bulgaria), *Ravnovesie/Balance* (Bourgas, Bulgaria), *Demetra/Demetra* (Bourgas, Bulgaria), *Union of Local Mayors at the Veliko Turnovo City Council* (Veliko Turnovo, Bulgaria), and *İnsan Kaynağını Geliştirme Vakfı/Human Resource Development Foundation* (Istanbul, Turkey). My thanks go to their staff members, who were very responsive to my requests and extremely helpful. The producers of *Face Down* gave me access to the film before it had wide distribution and for this I am grateful.

I have also benefited from exchanges and discussions with many colleagues, who merit recognition, such as the late Natalia Olshanskaya (Kenyon College), Jennifer Suchland and Wendy Hesford (both OSU), Stepanka Korytova (Indiana University), Emily Schuckman Matthews (San Diego State University), and Dina Iordanova (St. Andrews University, Scotland), to mention just a few. I am thankful to my Bulgarian collaborators, Roumiana Bozhinova and Ergyul Tair, scholars at the Bulgarian Academy of Sciences, for their expertise and time they dedicated to our project, a cross-cultural study of attitudes toward trafficking, published first in the *Bulgarian Journal of Psychology* and also here with modifications. Last but not least, my most avid discussant and critical reader, Luzmila Camacho Platero, deserves my greatest appreciation and gratitude.

Special acknowledgment goes to the anonymous peer-reviewers of the manuscript, who provided most constructive feedback. I particularly appreciate the help of Katie Lane, my research assistant, who patiently and painstakingly worked with me through many versions of various chapters to prepare this manuscript for publication. I am happy for the opportunity to recognize the exceptional professionalism of the editors at Central European University Press and thank them for their assistance.

I would not have been able to do any of what I do without the unconditional love of my wonderful (and large) family (Lorenzo, Lita, my mother, Maria, Christo, Kalina, and Katerina). They not only believe in me and support my work, but, more importantly, make sure I enjoy life!

Introduction

"Students watched the American film *Human Trafficking* with Mira Sorvino, so they can see how trafficking unfolds in real-life situations."

Social Club "Open Your Eyes" lesson plan (Resen, Bulgaria)

Now, at the beginning of the twenty-first century, policymakers and activists consider human trafficking to be one of the most dramatic challenges of the global world, alongside terrorism and drug trafficking. The phenomenon of human trafficking poses challenges and has consequences to national and international communities that can be lasting and more complex than the difficulties presented by the nuclear arms race. The US Government Trafficking in Persons Report (TIP) from 2014 states: "It is estimated that as many as 20 million men, women, and children around the world are victims of what is now often described with the umbrella term 'human trafficking.'" *The Palermo Protocol* definition has become the most widely accepted, recognized by active parties involved in combating trafficking, including the US Government. It describes "trafficking in persons" as:

the recruitment, transportation, transfer, harbouring or receipt of persons, by means of the threat or use of force or other forms of coercion, of abduction, of fraud, of deception, of the abuse of power or of a position of vulnerability or of the giving or receiving of payments or benefits to achieve the consent of a person having control over another person, for the purpose of exploitation. Exploitation shall include, at a minimum, the exploitation of the prostitution of others or other forms of sexual exploitation, forced labour or services, slavery or practices similar to slavery, servitude or the removal of organs. (United Nations, *Protocol to Prevent, Suppress and Punish Trafficking in Persons*, art. 3a.)

In the last decade, US (and global) television and cinema viewers have witnessed a persistent engagement with the topic of trafficking in popular shows such as *Criminal Minds*, *Law and Order: Special Victims Unit*, *CSI: NY*, *CSI: Miami*, *NCIS*, *NCIS: Los Angeles*, *The Mentalist*, and *American Crime*, among others. In 2012, CNN launched a campaign called "The Freedom Project" with a dedicated webpage (www.cnn.com/freedom) presenting reports, stories, and data on trafficking. As of January 2016, the project continues to document trafficking stories and experiences of survivors and combatting forces. CNN also broadcasts regular reports and documentaries on trafficking and screens a short clip advertising its Freedom Project. Powerful documentaries—Frontline's *Sex Slaves* (PBS, 2007), MSNBC's *Undercover: Sex Slaves* (2007), Al Jazeera's *Slavery: A 21st Century Evil* (2011), and National Geographic Channel's *21st Century Sex Slaves* (2012)—have also been repeatedly broadcast on US TV channels and are available online via iTunes. In addition, numerous recent feature films, such as *The Whistleblower* (Germany, Canada, US, 2010), *Taken* (France, UK, US, 2010), *Taken 2* (France, 2012), *Eastern Promises* (UK, Canada, US, 2007), *Trade* (Germany, US, 2007), *Broken Trail* (Canada, US, 2006), and Lifetime TV's *Human Trafficking* (Canada, US, 2005) have achieved popularity and relative box-office success.

The noticeable increase in the production of feature films, television dramas, and documentaries focusing on trafficking in people reveals both a social engagement on the part of journalists and filmmakers, as well as a broader public interest. These media reports and films, however, invite closer scrutiny, for the representation of trafficking and its violence can be as perilous as it is helpful in combating this twenty-first century major human rights violation. Although my analysis does not engage in depth with all of the discourses framing trafficking and particularly avoids the abolitionist one, it is worth mentioning here that some anti-trafficking campaigns of NGOs and community based (often faith driven) organizations intentionally and persistently conflate trafficking and prostitution to present the denigrating and dangerous aspects of both and to criminalize prostitution. Focusing on the analysis of film and media products, I acknowledge this ideological discourse but do not engage in detail in exposing its objectives.[1]

The US government employs feature films and media in its efforts to promote public awareness about modern slavery. In 2012, President Obama's administration published a report on the progress on combating trafficking in persons. Among numerous other measures, the Department of Health and Human Services distributed 772,328 materials for the Rescue & Restore Victims of Human Trafficking public awareness campaign and posted online, in English and Spanish, its Rescue & Restore training video *Look Beneath the Surface*. In the fall of 2016 and in the context of the US presidential election campaign, one of Hillary Clinton's nationwide advertisements featured her active involvement in the fight against human trafficking.

In 2007, the US government initiated a film outreach campaign to raise international awareness about the dangers of human trafficking, and US embassies around the world organized screenings of trafficking films for local audiences. This campaign, and the US embassies often participating in it—and understandably so—reached out and used locally produced films about trafficking.[2] East European cinemas and NGOs, for instance, similar to the Western world, have produced documentaries and feature films to raise awareness about trafficking. Since the collapse of state socialism in Eastern Europe, the region has been dramatically affected by trafficking, and it is not surprising that national media, cinemas, and NGOs also engage with the problem.

Considering the horrific impact of human trafficking and the difficulties governments and international communities have in reducing its disastrous effects on the most vulnerable people, prudent aware-

---

[1] For more on the various debates and discourses on trafficking, see Stephanie Limoncelli's *The Politics of Trafficking*.

[2] For more details on the US Embassy in Bulgaria and its involvement, see http://fsi.stanford.edu/sites/default/files/Antoaneta_Vassileva.pdf [last accessed: January 25, 2016].

ness campaigns appear to be an important tool in combatting trafficking. A latent consensus exists among NGOs, community organizations, governmental institutions, and film and media creators that screening trafficking is one of the most effective techniques for prevention and awareness. In 2008, The United Nations Global Initiative to Fight Human Trafficking (UN.GIFT) organized a Film Forum in Vienna dedicated to human trafficking. The Forum's catalog, distributed during the three-day long event opens with introductory words by Antonio Maria Costa, Executive Director of the United Nations Office on Drugs and Crime:

> The films that you are about to see may cause discomfort. In some cases viewer discretion is advised. But once you leave the cinema, don't close your eyes to the fate of children, women, and men who are drugged, threatened and beaten, and then exploited like disposable commodities whether as child soldiers, sex workers, or slave labourers... Every film on human trafficking sends a powerful message. All those messages together will mobilize the forces we need to make UN.GIFT a turning point in the fight against this form of modern-day slavery. (*Films on Human Trafficking. February 2008* 2008, 9)

Costa's emphasis on the power of film to affect the viewer reveals recent actions of engaging the media in the fight against trafficking. The second introduction to the Forum's catalogue, signed by UN.GIFT, similarly insists that: "stories, both positive and negative, told through film go straight into the heart" (2008, 13). Echoing this opinion, the curators of the Forum, Heidi Lobato and Mienno Liauw, claim that: "an essential part of a film as a medium is identification. It is much easier for us to identify with people who we can see" (2008, 19–20). These voices uniformly articulate the necessity of prudent media engagement in the eradication of trafficking.

At the same time, Costa's introduction also hints at the danger or the perilous effects of some films. Emma Thompson, the Oscar-winning British actress who created an effective anti-trafficking installation *Journey* and who joined forces with UN.GIFT, in an interview published in the Forum's catalogue expresses concerns about some of these aspects of screening trafficking: "Unfortunately, I think sometimes when you present things too graphically, people get frightened and they can't cope with the suffering" (2008, 16). Although said cautiously, Thompson suggests that violence and graphic bodily abuse are not always effective in achieving the necessary awareness and creating a socially engaged viewer.

Prevention and awareness campaigns often choose films with questionable qualities—films that can turn viewers away rather than evoke empathy and transformation, calling for action. The recent media interest in trafficking—primarily sex trafficking—has raised some awareness among policymakers and citizens, but it has also appealed to voyeuristic viewers. The UN.GIFT Film Forum's curators also acknowledge the increased media focus on sex trafficking, no doubt for its titillating aspect. When asked about this, Lobato responds: "I have noticed that, too; the majority of films concerns sexploitation, true. Sex sells, which might be one reason I suppose, despite how questionable it is in this case" (2008, 21). Undoubtedly, one agrees with Lobato's view, but it is necessary to stress here that human rights violations of a sexual nature are considered in general some of the most heinous and hideous crimes. While film and media representations of sexual abuse often mask titillating qualities, sexual crimes provoke strong outrage. In this respect, sex trafficking films can have the potential to generate engaged viewers who can become activists in the fight against trafficking and, at the same time, hide the risks of creating only voyeurs.

The discussion of the films that follows in this book exposes precisely this dilemma of screening trafficking—prudently necessary and at the same time perilous. In addition to the risks of using films in the prevention and awareness campaign mentioned briefly above, one can detect yet another danger—the ideological background of the creators and production companies of these films. Regardless of how sincerely all filmmakers engage with the subject of trafficking, certain sets of ideological inclinations always surface under closer scrutiny.

Whereas Africa, South and Central America, and Asia are also subject to the global scale of organized crime, and the human rights violations of trafficking and media in these regions also address the issue, my work investigates Western (including Western Europe, the US, and Canada) and primarily East European media products. I do this in an attempt to examine similarities and differences between these two types of productions, as well as to offer a more focused analysis on certain films rather than produce a survey of films worldwide on the topic of trafficking. More importantly, this structure allows me to explore not only the dynamics between the different approaches to reporting on trafficking, but also to problematize some ideological underpinnings of the representation of trafficking.

The Old/New East-West Divide

The way I organize and analyze films and media examples—divided into Western and Eastern—demands a brief discussion on the usage of the terms Western and Eastern. Despite the criticism Edward Said received for his book *Orientalism*, his work powerfully called attention to Eurocentric or Occidental views of the world, views that construct others—in Said's analysis, Oriental others—as inferior. The psychological and cultural othering, however, was discussed long before Said, and here it is worth mentioning Mikhail Bakhtin. In the early 1920s, Bakhtin maintained that the subject's knowledge of itself or the world is impossible without the other, because meaning occurs in discourse where consciousnesses meet (Bakhtin 1990, 89).

Although the cultural construction of Eastern Europe as a less developed or backward (politically, economically, and culturally) region was cemented and received new connotations during the Cold War, the very notion of Eastern Europe as "different" was invented in the eighteenth century, when, as Larry Wolff maintains, Eastern Europe was accepted geographically as part of Europe but not quite European (1994, 7). In his book *Uses of the Other*, Iver Neumann similarly develops the argument that Eastern Europe is perceived as "other" (among various "others") for Europe's superior self-image. Adding to the studies of othering, Maria Todorova convincingly details the European process of othering the Balkans, first in her article "The Balkans: From Discovery to Invention," and later in her seminal book *Imagining the Balkans*. She opens her article with the following statement:

> By the beginning of the twentieth century Europe has added to its repertoire of *Schimpfwörter*, or disparagements, a new one which turned out to be more persistent than others with centu-

ries old traditions. "Balkanization" not only had come to denote the parcelization of large and viable political units but also had become a synonym for a reversion to the tribal, the backward, the primitive, the barbarian. (1994, 453)

The perception of Eastern Europe has not been static and homogenous, for, as Todorova proves, the Balkans evoked different imaginary from that of East Central Europe. Scholars increasingly turn their attention to the processes of cultural "othering," and the field of "othering" has expanded in the last decade to include studies on the construction of Eastern Europe and its modifications both in the past and after the collapse of the socialist system. In 1994, Michael Kennedy, arguing about the relationship between the West and Eastern Europe during the early years of the transition period, called attention to the transformation of the market and of democracy into "master narratives" (1994, 2–4). In *On the East-West Slope*, Attila Melegh details the discursive structure and cognitive order of differentiation on the descending scale of "civilization to barbarism," a structure that appears in various forms of knowledge, from political to popular (2007, 9).

In film studies, several works explore the cultural constructs or perceptions of Western and Eastern Europe as different from each other. Dina Iordanova's *Cinema of the Other Europe* contributes to the knowledge of East Central European film and culture, pointing out that East European film remains largely excluded from the concept of European cinema. More directly engaging with the cinematic depictions of Russians in Hollywood films as others or of Americans in Russian films, Tony Shaw and Denise Youngblood's *Cinematic Cold War: The American and Soviet Struggle for Hearts and Minds* and Helena and Margaret B. Goscilo's *Fade from Red: The Cold War Ex-Enemy in Russian and American Film 1990–2005* detail how the changing portrayals of Soviets/Russians or Americans are often motivated by political or market factors. While Shaw and Youngblood reveal how Cold War propaganda played out on the screen, the Goscilos investigate how cinema continued to shape the image of the other after the Cold War ended. My earlier work *Pride and Panic: Russian Imagination of the West in Post-Soviet Film* focuses on Russia's national identity constructs and the ways the image of the West as the other plays an important role in Russians' understanding of themselves.

East European otherness proves to be an enduring quality and subject of discussion in Western media, and the film production of trafficking offers yet another example.[3] The most recent instance of the long-lasting perception of Eastern Europe as the less civilized other of Western Europe emerged during the refugee crisis in the fall of 2015, when Western media outlets such as CNN, BBC, and Euronews persistently framed South Eastern and Central European states as xenophobic and incapable of handling the refugee crisis. (Un)surprisingly, only a few months later, in January of 2016, when West European states had to tackle the migrant situation on their own territories, xenophobic attitudes began to surface and new border controls were introduced, which did not receive the media coverage of the East European manifestations of the same response.

During the eighteenth and nineteenth centuries, Western Europe assumed the central role in this type of construction, which positions the West as superior, both culturally and morally. In the last century, the United States similarly imagined itself as a model to be followed and emulated by other, lesser-developed regions in the world, Eastern Europe, Russia, and the Balkans included. This division was undoubtedly fueled by Cold War rhetoric and accompanying worldviews.

These types of binary perceptions of the world are evident in Western films and media products on trafficking, and I critically investigate the differences between Western and South Eastern European media productions. Although the Western creators of these products are socially engaged filmmakers and activists, I contend that the West's perception of its cultural and economic dominance negatively affects the accuracy of their trafficking representations.

To complicate matters further, the division between the West and Eastern Europe hides the complex dynamics and tension between the demand (West) and the supply (Eastern Europe) sides of the trafficking process. It has been documented (US TIP Report, Suchland

---

[3] It suffices to mention that a movement to recast "Central Europe" as a separate and unique region emerged forcefully in the late 1980s and especially in the 1990s, which required the othering of other regions and countries like Russia and the Balkans (Comisso and Gutierrez 2004, Neumann 1999). For Russia's construction of its own others, see Norris and Torlone 2008, Hutchings 2008, and Hashamova 2015.

2015, to name just two sources) that the trade in human beings follows the economic model of supply and demand, as humans from countries with lower living standards and economic/political problems function as supply regions (people seek better opportunities abroad and become trafficked), while the more prosperous and developed West demands cheap labor and sexual services, thus creating an opportunity for organized crime and abuse to flourish. Most of the trafficked people end up in the Western part of the world. It is not surprising that, alarmed by the scale of the trafficking, Western media and cinema have taken a proactive position to raise awareness and fight this modern slavery. Its perilous involvement is being critically addressed here.

Violence and Trauma

The matter of people's activism (social participation, recognition, and prevention of trafficking), and especially activism related to representations of sex trafficking is a complex process that involves a series of tensions. Ideological background notwithstanding, binary perspectives lie at the heart of the public perception of the trafficking experience: individual and collective identifications, reality and representation, and facts and myths. My research shows that whereas governmental and institutional responses are critical to the prevention of and the battle against trafficking, so, too, is public understanding of how traumatic experiences are represented and understood culturally, and how film and other cultural forms can help people and communities transform representations of individual trauma into a collective ethical imperative. The representation of sex trafficking and its use requires a more complex analysis and understanding, for it hides latent conflicts between evoking empathy (catharsis) and inciting titillation. So, to the ideological discussion that frames the representation of trafficking in Western and South East European productions, one can add the complexities of representing violence and trauma, as Thompson suggests above. As a humanist who straddles several disciplines, I conduct research that combines cinematic and media analysis, social psychology, political ideology, and cultural and gender studies. As most films analyzed here depict the servitude and violation of women, gender and feminist concepts guide my analysis. In order to probe whether the violence and trauma depicted in most films of sex trafficking reach the viewer, I borrow from trauma and cinema theory, especially the way it defines possible positions of the viewer vis-à-vis visual trauma.

This book examines media materials used by the public, NGOs, and governments in the United States, Western Europe, and South Eastern Europe to raise awareness about trafficking. Capital and economics, as well as artistic skills and professional understandings— including the operational concepts of marketing and audiences—influence the final media or cinematic product. Content analysis of feature films and documentaries—especially the former—sheds light on these relationships. Producers and the production aspect of sex trafficking film and media directly or indirectly determine the choice of genres, the construction of stereotypes, and the representation of traumatic images. My content examination of media materials and films reveals that most Western, South East European, and co-productions construct stereotypes. Significantly, however, these films display different stereotypes depending on their production origin and priorities.

The Gaze and the Violated Body

In the analysis of the construction of trafficking victims, perpetrators, and rescuers, I am guided to a certain degree by the concepts of the gaze and the look. The term "gaze" can lead some readers to Jacques Lacan's claim that the gaze *qua object a* prevents the subject from knowing what is there beyond appearance (Lacan 1981, 67–78). The free-floating gaze ultimately attached to the visual is there to unveil the unreliable nature of appearance. As Italian film scholar Fabio Vighi contends, "cinema's own reflexive/self referential nature offers us a unique chance to investigate the correlation between what we see and permeate with meaning and the displaced element that governs it most secretly" (2006, 34). The use of the gaze in this book differs from Lacan's de-essentializing force, as the free-floating gaze connected to *object a*, situated beyond appearance. Feminist scholars have drifted from such function of the gaze, for they claim that "Lacan's gaze cannot be used to analyze sexual difference because it allows no differential analysis of mastery and subjection—everyone is subjected to a gaze which is outside" (Doane 1990, 55).[4]

In exploring the interrelatedness and odd dynamics of cultural othering, I utilize two interrelated terms, "gaze" and "look," introduced to film theory and more specifically to feminist film theory by Laura Mulvey in her groundbreaking essay, "Visual Pleasure and Narrative Cinema." Since then, other theorists have developed and differentiated the two terms. Here, I follow in the steps of E. Ann Kaplan, who was interested in the "looking relation" and its historical, cultural, and psychoanalytic implications (Kaplan 1997).[5] I use the term "look" to indicate a relation and a process implying desire to know and curiosity about the other, while the "gaze" designates the extreme anxiety and fears that preclude knowledge (Kaplan 1997, xvi–xxi). The look is more interested in the object, whereas the gaze, consumed by its own anxieties, impedes the (learning) process and prohibits a relationship with the object. "The object is a threat to the subject's autonomy and security and thus must be placed, rationalized and, by a circuitous route, denied. [...] The gaze, finally, for me connotes an active subject versus a passive object" (Kaplan 1997, xviii). These two concepts shed light on how trafficking films construct the victims and their realities, the perpetrators, and the forces that combat trafficking. Since this book explores Western and East European production of trafficking films, distinguishing between gaze and look and, moreover, associating the (male) gaze with the Western (presumed superior) gaze, which according to Kaplan cannot be separated within Western patriarchal culture, proves helpful in pointing out the desired privileged status the West assumes in the depiction of trafficking.

---

[4] For more on the discussion around the use of the "gaze" and especially the feminist approach to film and psychoanalysis, see Doane (1990, 46–64) and Kaplan (1990, 1–24).

[5] Although Kaplan acknowledges Jane Gaines' contribution to the looking relation, the latter mainly critiqued feminist theory for not addressing the issues of race and its connection to psychoanalytic scholarship. For my argument, the most productive use of the "look" was developed by Judith Mayne and especially Kaplan, who critically and productively incorporates psychoanalysis in her use of the "look," as she differentiates it from the "gaze" in her exploration of gendered and Western imperial constructions in film.

The gaze that orchestrates the field of vision carries with it the power to subjugate subjects—in the case of trafficking films exposing the sexual exploitation mainly of women and children—to the position of victimized objects whose bodies undergo brutality, captured by the camera. On a technical level, the gaze is aligned with the agency (or the immediate substitute) of power that ideologically controls and organizes the field of vision.

Media and the Viewer

Following the axis of production-text-audience, my study demonstrates that while production and text matter, the viewer also participates in the creation of meaning. There is a distinct interconnectedness between the cultural/national identifications of viewers (religious environment and belonging, for instance) and how these identifications might alter the perception of trafficking on the one hand, and, on the other, the media environments, which in turn shape attitudes toward trafficking. The complex interrelation between cultural identifications, which determine attitudes, and media, which molds opinions, demands exploration and is one of the foci of this book. I develop the hypothesis that the cultural, political, and gender backgrounds of audiences in various regions of the world affect the perception of trafficking and the effectiveness of prevention campaigns. One of the major factors which underlines the differences in the perception of trafficking in the US and Eastern Europe, for instance, lies in the nature of the relationship between these two areas—a relationship defined by the supply and demand model and by the perception of otherness.

The national, cultural, and gender identities of audiences shape their responses to media products and influence the creation of meaning. Unlike media studies scholar John Fiske, who argues for the dissolution of the concepts "text" and "audience," I believe that it is not productive to abandon them entirely, but to study them interdependently (Fiske 1989). In my view, only a comprehensive analysis of these products—an analysis that explores the tensions between production, text, and audience—provides a constructive critique of the usefulness of media materials in anti-trafficking campaigns. My approach to the study of audiences combines field work at NGOs in Macedonia and Bulgaria (examining their archives and reports which focus on their use of anti-trafficking media in prevention campaigns) and sociological surveys (testing attitudes toward trafficking in the United States and Bulgaria), as case studies revealing differences based on national, cultural, and gender backgrounds.

In the last two decades, human trafficking has been examined from various perspectives: cultural theorists, political scientists, and sociologists address the political, economic, and legal aspects of trafficking; some scholars analyze the problem in the framework of transnational crime and criminal justice; others study human trafficking in the context of globalization; and some investigate the complex debates of trafficking and anti-trafficking policies and the way international NGOs participate in them. Scholarship on media/film and trafficking, however, is still severely lacking. It mainly consists of a few articles and the tri-authored *Moving People, Moving Images: Cinema and Trafficking in the New Europe* (2010), which aims primarily to raise theoretical questions and provide a filmography (sporadic on East European media and NGO materials). A considerable portion of *Moving People, Moving Images* and the films it discusses addresses the problem of migrant workers in feature films, whereas my work analyzes mostly sex trafficking films, documentaries, and NGO media products.

Structure

The book is divided in two parts: the viewer and the representation. Chapter 1 briefly outlines the economic, political and cultural conditions as related to trafficking in South Eastern Europe and the US, arguing that the differences in these conditions shape varying perceptions of trafficking. The legacy of the Yugoslav Wars and the difficult transition in Bulgaria from socialist to capitalist economy affecting negatively and disproportionately ethnic minorities to a certain degree determine the functioning of this region as a donor and transit area for trafficking. Contrary to these conditions, the developed economy of the US defines this country as a destination region, although matters are more complex than that. The facts about the US strong economy are intertwined with myths about the land of endless opportunities that obscure the development of domestic trafficking and, conse-

quently, impact perceptions about US trafficking victims and survivors. Expanding the argument that viewers' national backgrounds
affect their understanding of this criminal and human rights violation,
this chapter also examines social attitudes toward trafficking and asks
whether they fluctuate according to national and cultural belonging.
Sociological and socio-psychological studies on attitudes toward trafficking are included.

Chapter 2 describes NGOs' film media campaigns and offers an
analysis of viewers' responses. My interest in viewers and their reactions to trafficking films began during my work in NGOs in Macedonia
and Bulgaria, while I was studying NGOs' reports and media materials. In conversations with staff from these NGOs about their prevention campaigns, I learned that films are screened to at-risk groups (students from orphanages or economically depressed regions), members
of the police force, and judges. After screenings, the NGOs' social
workers conduct discussions with the viewers. More intriguingly,
I realized that the viewers' reactions to Western and locally produced
films differ and I began exploring these differences, as recorded in the
NGOs reports and activities' notes. Through content analysis of these
documents, I construct a narrative about Macedonian and Bulgarian
viewers' responses to anti-trafficking films.

My investigation of viewers' attitudes toward trafficking culmi-
nated in a collaboration with colleagues from the Bulgarian Academy
of Sciences, Roumiana Bozhinova and Ergyul Tair. Together we
designed and executed a study to test attitudes towards trafficking
among Bulgarian and American (Ohio State University) students
based both on their overall knowledge and on a film shown to them.
Chapter 3 presents this comparative investigation. My work logically
unfolded into a bigger project, which studies the content and aesthetic
characteristics of Western and Eastern European films exploring the
phenomenon of trafficking.

In Part Two, Chapter 4 pays attention to the funding aspects
of Western films and how these aspects influence the results.
Globalization has been understood as the unparalleled expansion of
transnational capital advanced by the collapse of Soviet-style socialism
(Kang 1998). But globalization also sets up the structural framework
for analyzing what happens in today's world, and is therefore used here
in more precise (dialectical) terms: it refers to an ideology of a global

(capitalist) market dictated by the West and mainly by the United States—the triumphant "winner" of the Cold War and (until recently, when Vladimir Putin defied international agreements and US objections in the annexation of Crimea) the unchallenged superpower in the world—ideology that determines the regulations not only for free trade but also for moral and cultural values (Kapur 1998). Slavoj Žižek writes: "The passage from actually existing Socialism to actually existing capitalism in Eastern Europe brought about a series of comic reversals of sublime democratic enthusiasm into the ridiculous" (2000, 205). The West impatiently waited for and instigated democratic changes in Russia and Eastern Europe because it wanted political pluralism and free-market economies—that is, new territory for the expansion of its capital. In turn, the Eastern Europeans, after idolizing and dreaming about prosperous democracies, have faced difficult transitions, marked by poverty as well as by cultural and economic colonization. The gaps that developed after the collapse of the Berlin Wall on both sides of the Iron Curtain—gaps between expectations and the economic, political, and social realities that unfolded—still shape the perceptions these societies have of each other. The new economies of developed and underdeveloped regions, as well as the old expectations still harbored by communities on both sides of the divide, have driven the phenomenon of trafficking and its boom in Europe.

Trafficking in people brutally illustrates these dynamics and reveals how the West and Eastern Europe have occupied the two sides of Karl Marx's formula of demand and supply, in which human bodies and labor are in demand and impoverished communities in Eastern Europe supply them, as human bodies stand for commodities. The transformation of capital to money follows Marx's formula M(oney)-C(ommodity)-M(oney), in which people become the commodity. My analysis of films such as the US TV Lifetime drama *Human Trafficking* and the British television miniseries *Sex Traffic* (UK/Canada, 2004), which are entirely devoted to sex trafficking cases, exemplifies how Western productions portray the demand and supply side. While *Sex Traffic* critically addresses the involvement of the West in not only purchasing sex and women's bodies but also the corporate participation in organized crime, *Human Trafficking* focuses on the criminal activity of one Russian businessman/gangster who operates a trafficking ring in New York. This difference speaks of the producers' tendencies to satisfy audiences' expectations, to name just one factor. In the United States, the film was created as a criminal/police drama in which "good" prevails over "evil," the gangster is killed and most of the victims released. In England, where the miniseries aired on BBC Four, a more critical and complex approach to Western involvement and participation in trafficking was offered with a sophisticated network of corporate and private agencies all connected to trafficking.[6] At the same time, the big screen production *Eastern Promises*, with an estimated budget of $25,000,000, which grossed over $20,000,000 in the first three months of worldwide screenings, also centers on one Russian former criminal (*vor v zakone*) and current businessman in London, whose family traffics and abuses young Russian women. Although the danger (in the face of the Russian criminal family) coming from Russia to "peaceful" London lurks through the simple crime drama, David Cronenberg's directing style (memorable from *History of Violence*) creates a more complex moral drama in which the tension between the West and the East in today's global world of capital and values becomes a dominating force.

Human Trafficking and *Sex Traffic* similarly depict the economic realities in Eastern Europe as the conditions driving the supply side of the economic model; material deprivation and desperation motivate East European women to seek better opportunities in Western Europe. If the presentation of these economic realities and the dream of Western opulence is a bit sketchy in the abovementioned two films, then *Import/Export* (Austria, France, Germany, 2007) and especially *Lilya 4-ever* (Sweden, Denmark, 2002) dedicate considerable narrative time to the description of Ukraine's and Russia's respective failed economic and social structures after the collapse of the Soviet Union. It is unsurprising that with the strong emphasis on the dark and depressing realities in Russia's provinces, *Lilya 4-ever* did not appeal to Russian viewers.

Unlike the films mentioned above, *Broken Trail* (Canada, US, 2006) and *Taken* (France, 2008) follow a different model of the supply and demand side of trafficking. The narrative of *Broken Trail*, set in 1898, presents the intersection of a classical western and a typical trafficking story. Two cowboys, who are delivering a herd of horses,

---

[6] This issue of what demand countries in the West choose to portray in feature films, as well as these films in particular, are discussed further in Chapter 4.

become the unwilling protectors and saviors of five Chinese trafficked women. The territory of supply this time is moved farther east, beyond Eastern Europe, to China. However, the battle of good versus evil persists with the inevitable and comforting moral victory. *Taken*, on the other hand, locates both the demand and the supply in the West, as the daughter of a former CIA agent is kidnapped in France, abused, and passed from trafficker to trafficker. The East European link in this trafficking film, however, is not left unattended: by implicating Albanian criminals operating in France, the narrative titillates and fuels Western anxieties of the other, who is corrupting and endangering its social structures and values. Although these films reveal a diverse model of the demand and supply sides of trafficking, some underlying patterns exist: Eastern Europe is mostly depicted as the supplier of both female flesh for the pleasure of Western men and organized criminals who have infiltrated the US and Western Europe. Although questioned in films like *Sex Traffic*, the allusion to the superior morality of the West dominates the films.

Paying attention to the selection of material (trafficking cases) and data presented, the second part of Chapter 4 examines media reports on trafficking and documentaries broadcast on television. I study the CNN International campaign "Freedom Project: Ending Modern-Day Slavery" and other documentaries and question their quest for objectivity and truthfulness. As film theorist Claire Johnston states: "There is no such thing as unmanipulated writing, filming or broadcasting [...] If we accept that cinema involves the production of signs, the idea of non-intervention is pure mystification. The sign is always a product. What the camera in fact grasps is the 'natural' world of the dominant ideology" (1985, 213–214). In a way, I investigate the signs of the dominant ideology in these media products and the spin they give to trafficking. Documentaries subject to my analysis include Frontline's *Sex Slaves*, Al Jazeera's *Slavery: A 21st Century Evil*, CNN's *Not My Life*, and the Rescue and Restore organization's *Look Beneath the Surface*.

Moving away from the Western gaze, Chapter 5 concentrates on East European feature films and NGO-commissioned short films and media materials. Unlike the Western films, which are commercially made and later used by organizations and activists, some of the films in this chapter are sponsored by NGOs. The interest of commercial films in the demand regions varies, but one can argue that even if the

Western role to the boon of trafficking is acknowledged and critiqued, the films' main preoccupation centers on supply areas' conditions and reasons. With the exception of the Russian production *All the Things We Dreamed of for so Long* (1997), which blames the moral corruption of Russian youths who become victims of prostitution (or trafficking) and money entirely onto the West, other films such as *Spare Parts* (Slovenia, 2004), *Lady Zee* (Bulgaria, 2005), *The Melon Route* (Croatia, 2006), *Sisters* (Serbia, 2011), and *Face Down* (Bulgaria-France, 2015) prefer to tackle the moral erosion and social and economic devastation of these East European societies as a result of the transition from collapsed socialism to unstable democracies. Matters are usually more complex than a simple explanation of motivations that drive East European filmmakers to probe national social and ethical conditions, and although I offer some educated guesses about these motivations, it is important to stress that for a more complete understanding of trafficking films, one needs to know that a different set of factors shape Western and East European cinematic productions.

While these films strongly convey the notion that people are transformed into commodities, some of them explore the smuggling of illegal migrants and do not engage in titillating the viewer by showing female nudity and flesh. There are exceptions, however, like *All That We Dreamed of for so Long* and *Lady Zee*, but even they grant agency to female sexuality, as these films' scenes of sexual intercourse with graphic nudity are not part of the women's trafficking experience and thus can be interpreted as empowering (to) them. More interestingly, three films, *The Melon Route, Sisters,* and *Face Down,* expose Eastern Europe as not only a donor or source (supply) region, but also as an active and willing collaborator in the global trafficking operation: local men as well as women transport and traffic illegal foreign migrants (African, Chinese, and Arabic) or their own community people through the Balkans to Europe.[7] Although the West is still presented as a driving force or destination, these films address the complicity and moral degradation of their own societies. Chapter 5 offers a thorough analysis of the way both local traffickers and trafficked persons are depicted. The resolution suggested

---

[7] Similarly, the 2005 documentary *Inhuman Traffic* (presented by Angelina Jolie) features two women who were sold into slavery by a fellow citizen; one by her neighbor and one by her boyfriend.

by these East European films diverges from the mostly upbeat outcome of Western productions, in which "goodness" triumphs.

I also examine sponsored films and media clips particularly created for and dedicated to the prevention of trafficking, as I attempt to decipher the "signs of dominant ideology." In the center of my analysis are short videos, animation clips, and posters produced by local artists and usually commissioned by NGOs in the Balkans. They, too, however, received some financial support from Western agents, even if indirectly, through the funds obtained by local NGOs working with or on these films. In these cases, the picture of sponsorship becomes more complicated and I bear these complexities in mind.

In Chapter 6, I study the possible effects that traumatic images (mostly rape scenes) in trafficking films can have on the viewer. Focusing primarily on transnational productions, I analyze how films depict the trauma of the violated body and how viewers are affected by such traumatic images. I contend that alongside the images of violated bodies, these films can evoke local (East European) viewers' identification and empathy only if the cultural context of these representations is complete, accurate, and respectful of the local culture. To Western viewers, these films present exoticized East European conditions, and although traumatic images might evoke empathy, at the same time these films perpetuate stereotypes. Utilizing concepts of cinema and trauma theory referring to possible positions of the spectator vis-à-vis distressing visuals, I investigate the effectiveness of the cruelty and violence represented in trafficking films and how they do or do not expand the conceptual horizons of the viewer.

The study of the audience and the production aspects of films, together with the examination of social attitudes towards trafficking and their cultural motivation, draws a complex picture of the media's involvement in this modern slavery. The analysis of these films and media materials leads me to believe that although they are created by socially involved filmmakers, they cater to certain ideological and economic interests, which can be an impediment to the effectiveness of these films. To be fair, I acknowledge that all awareness campaigns matter and are efficient to a certain degree, but I also stress that activists, NGOs, and governments often select these products too casually, without a critical understanding of the hidden messages that these products transmit.

PART ONE

The Viewer

CHAPTER 1

Social, Political, and Cultural Conditions Affecting Trafficking and Its Perception

Although trafficking is a global phenomenon whose core nature is identical all over the world, local conditions define the specifics of trafficking—the way people become its victims as well as how the phenomenon is perceived. Why do the social, political, and economic conditions of viewers matter for their comprehension of anti-trafficking film and video materials? They matter and should be understood because they drive the creation as well as the reception of cultural products on the topic of trafficking which, in turn, have the potential to inform policy.

Arjun Appadurai's *Modernity at Large*, very well received in the 1990s, argues that the global cultural economy of that time should no longer be comprehended through the old model of center-periphery, because the forces of globalization created new forms of cultural dimensions defined with the suffix "scape" (ethnoscape, mediascape, technoscape, financescape, and ideoscape). In his discussion of the public perception and knowledge of cricket in India, and how it was shaped by vernacular literature, radio, and television, for example, he contends that these mass-mediated forms "have created a public that is extremely large, literate in many different senses in the subtleties of the sport, and can bring to cricket passions generated by reading, hearing, and seeing" (Appadurai 1996, 102). Following this belief in the flow of "scapes" and the almost universal access to mass media images, and extending it to anti-trafficking media products, viewers around the globe should understand the nature and causes of trafficking in an identical way, for they encounter the same or similar mediascapes and become similarly "literate" in the subject.

However, my argument so far shows that viewers' attitudes toward trafficking, even though influenced by mediascapes (for example, the international understanding of the conventions of the action genre and the wide distribution in Eastern Europe of such action films as *Taken*), cannot exist independently of local conditions grounded in viewers' national, economic, and cultural backgrounds. On the contrary, various markers of identity, ranging from national and economic to religious and gender, shape the collective perception.

While Appadurai contends that the mass media and mass migration have led to the instability of national and cultural identities and urges his readers to "think ourselves beyond the nation" (1996, 158), he also discusses the production of locality, which should be understood "as primarily relational and contextual rather than as scalar and spatial" (178). Even though Appadurai advances the idea that globalization is acutely historical, irregular, and, paradoxically, a localizing process—as locality is a structure of feeling caused by forms of international activity—my study reveals that the dynamics between the local conditions and mediascapes (to use his term) are more complex than his argument presents and excellently exemplify the tension between global mediascapes and their local comprehension. More importantly, I contend that local identities can often dominate the comprehension of a global phenomenon like trafficking despite the public's similar "literacy" about it.

In this chapter I outline some differences in the economic, political, cultural, and historical conditions that define trafficking in Bulgaria, Macedonia, and the United States, and examine how these conditions (in)directly contribute to people's views on trafficking. I also offer social studies data and socio-psychological research findings about attitudes towards trafficking in Bulgaria and the US, showing that while the two groups share some attitudes, their opinions also vary on certain aspects of trafficking. The trafficking conditions in Macedonia and Bulgaria are similar insofar as these two countries function mainly as countries of source and transit for trafficked women and children; what distinguishes them is the legacy of Yugoslavia and its collapse which, to a considerable degree, shapes organized crime in Macedonia.

Bulgaria

In Bulgaria, during the period of Soviet socialism, the lack of communication and the inability for people to travel freely helped communist propaganda to demonize the West. The Iron Curtain was more than a dividing line; it was the boundary beyond which socialist people were not allowed to see. They were left to fantasize about a forbidden "Garden of Eden" ripe with sinful temptation. Thus, the West was simultaneously demonized and desired. The isolation of Bulgaria, which lasted for many years, still affects ordinary people's lives. In rural areas, the lack of information and a realistic idea of Western societies feed the myth of the idealized forbidden fruit of happiness and prosperity. While young people who are targeted by traffickers know very little, even nothing, about the ways state socialism structured people's fantasies, they, living in underdeveloped areas with no economic and social opportunities, experience the lures of the West without any accurate information about conditions there.

Undoubtedly, there is in Bulgaria a slowly emerging middle class of professionals, but also a dangerous increase in poverty—especially in certain regions and among ethnic communities of Roma and Turks in the country—that has been well documented (Todorova, 1999; Ghodsee, 2010). In recent years, Bulgaria is consistently defined as the poorest country in the European Union (EU). According to the trafficking case records of Animus Association in Sofia, one of the survivors who sought their services told them that a kind and generous young man or "loverboy" lured her with chocolates and the promise of a job, and she ended up being trafficked to the Netherlands. Even if some (mistakenly) choose to attribute the responsibility of this case to the woman's naïveté, the lack of education/knowledge among local populations as a factor and the temptations of the West as motivation are undeniable. Economic desperation, low living standards, and a lack of opportunities for young people are the most powerful driving forces behind trafficking.

For a long time, state institutions have denied the existence of trafficking. Pressed by new Western partners in the process of integration into the EU and by some non-governmental organizations in the country, politicians have recognized the scale of the problem. In

2008, the Bulgarian government established a National Commission for Combating Trafficking in Human Beings (NCCTHB) of the Ministry of the Interior. According to their data, Bulgaria holds third place in Europe for the number of citizens trafficked abroad and is mainly a donor/source and transit country. NCCTHB outlines several preventive programs, commissions sociological surveys, and coordinates all activities of the government related to trafficking. After a long and detailed explanation of the difficulties and complexities of collecting data on trafficking, the statistics show that for 2009, there were 297 Bulgarians trafficked abroad (NCCTHB). At the same time, the Bulgarian media states that 10,000 Bulgarians are trafficked abroad annually (Ekov, 2009). The shocking discrepancy in the data is not unusual for human trafficking, as media tends to sensationalize the problem, while government reports only mention the documented cases, with perhaps hundreds of others unregistered and unknown.

According to the US Department of State's 2011 annual report, women and children are subjected to sex trafficking within Bulgaria particularly in resort areas and border towns. Ethnic Roma women, children, and men are more vulnerable to being trafficked. Bulgaria made trafficking for sexual exploitation and forced labor illegal in Article 159 (a, b and d) of its Criminal Code with penalties between two and fifteen years in prison. In 2010, the government identified 558 victims of trafficking; the police performed 160 new trafficking investigations including 11 labor trafficking investigations, compared to 149 sex trafficking (USDOS 2010). Since 2009, there has been an increase in sentenced trafficking offenders and investigations against police officers. However, there are many reports of trafficking-related complicity among government officials. Although one cannot deny the efforts of the Bulgarian government to combat trafficking, one should also note the enormous discrepancy between the numbers of trafficked people in different reports, as noted above. This inconsistency, no doubt, contributes to the overall ambiguous attitudes of Bulgarians toward trafficking.

Below I present some of the findings of social studies research commissioned by NCCTHB. As part of the national campaign "Trafficking in Human Beings: Time for Action," a class about human trafficking was conducted in many schools. Students and teachers from over 3,000 schools in Bulgaria sent 140,000 feedback forms: 7,837 by teachers and 133,189 by students. The main part of the recommendations focuses on the manner of the visualization of the topic. Teachers prefer video materials, documentaries, or scientific films, thinking that young people perceive visual materials much better than written text or lectures, and that such presentations will achieve an even higher involvement of the students (NCCTHB 2009). Undoubtedly, these results support my argument about the significance of media materials and the emphasis my work places on the careful selection of these materials.

In April 2008, Mediana Agency conducted a qualitative sociological survey, commissioned by NCCTHB, with four focus groups of young people between eighteen and thirty-five years of age. The title of the study was "Trafficking in Human Beings – Connotations, Meanings, Attitude and Expectations of Institutions." The results reveal interesting and inaccurate beliefs. In general, the concept of "trafficking in human beings" is associated primarily with the "export" of Bulgarians abroad or of foreigners passing through Bulgaria. To many participants, the concept is too vague and includes "anything illegal." The participants in the study show evasive reactions to the question "Is trafficking in human beings possible within the country?" "Maybe" is the predominant answer. Trafficking in Bulgarians is perceived as something that is not right, unfair. However, when trafficking involves foreigners in Bulgaria, attitudes change. "It is their own fault" is the predominant answer (NCCTHB April 2008). This attitude warrants further discussion. A possible reason for the more sympathetic view of Bulgarian trafficked persons compared to foreign nationals can be attributed to the high level of unemployment in Bulgaria and the overall desire of young people to seek career opportunities abroad, attempts which make them more susceptible to traffickers. Interestingly, the participants in the focus groups apparently sympathize with such efforts, for they imagine themselves in similar desperate situations. This sentiment, however, is not observed when foreign citizens are involved. Women trafficked to and through Bulgaria usually belong to states of the former Soviet Union and their economic conditions are reported as even worse than the Bulgarian ones. But the identification of Bulgarians appears to occur on a national/cultural level and not on an economic one.

In the same year, Mediana Agency conducted a quantitative sociological survey among 1,502 people over eighteen years of age under the title "Public Opinion and Public Attitudes toward Trafficking in Human Beings." The concept of "trafficking in human beings" has a negative connotation, but, significantly, one in four people are unclear about what it means. In one of the risk groups—young people with low education—the percentage of those who do not know what trafficking means is exactly 45 percent. At the same time, one in seven young people in Bulgaria are potential victims of trafficking: 13 percent state that they have plans to immigrate abroad in the next two to three years. Trafficking in human beings is mostly associated with sexual exploitation (forced prostitution), followed by labor exploitation and organ trade. This increased awareness of sex trafficking compared to labor or organ trafficking is no doubt attributed to the media information responders receive about trafficking. Circular forces are at play here; that is, viewers' greater interest in sex trafficking leads to media's stronger attention to it, which results in viewers' limited knowledge about other forms of trafficking, such as labor and organ. This conclusion reveals yet again the two aspects of representing trafficking, prudent and perilous, advisable and risky.

Most of the survey participants believe that trafficking occurs only when victims suffer physical abuse (forced prostitution and forced "bondage" of illegal workers). However, when trafficked people do not suffer physically, public opinion does not consider this trafficking at all. This view reminds the reader of the prevailing opinion that rape occurs only when the victim is physically battered. Two-thirds of the participants (more than 70 percent among young people) do not see anything wrong with someone becoming an "illegal" worker abroad. In other words, they do not perceive any danger of illegal workers being exploited and financially manipulated by employers. Significantly, more than half of the participants do not blame the trafficked people and believe that they have been misled and deceived because they are poorly educated, impoverished, and struggling to make a living. Yet, when it comes to sexual exploitation, public opinion (36 percent) is more likely to "blame" those who engaged in prostitution. It appears that in the mind of the Bulgarians surveyed, the women who end up trafficked in the sex industry do not try "to make a living." Passing judgment and dividing trafficked persons on the basis of moral convictions of how one can make a living reveals patriarchal and sexist views that have been cultivated in Bulgarian society. In addition, this opinion suggests projecting the blame only to the victim and not to the male consumer of her services.

38 percent of participants below the age of thirty-five are convinced that immigration is a good solution to their financial problems. In the at-risk group of young uneducated people, this share is 48 percent, and one-third of them are representatives of the Roma community. 21 percent of young people see European countries as places without poverty. These opinions clearly show the myths about the West that still persist in Bulgaria, despite the twenty-five-year-long process of democratization and opening to the West.

In her work on emerging poverty in Bulgaria, Sasha Todorova finds a positive correlation between poverty and low education, and locates it mainly in ethnic Roma communities. She notes that among the poverty risk groups in Bulgaria are "[d]ifferentiated ethnic groups (among the Gypsies we witness the closest correlation between ethnic descent and poverty), comprising 19.1 percent of the group but only 3.8 percent of the entire population. [...] They are poorly educated (57.8 percent of them have not finished primary school)" (Todorova, 1999, 83–84). Considering these statistics, it is unsurprising that Roma constitute a main trafficking risk group. Although the state has taken some steps in integrating the Roma community, these measures are ineffective and Roma are still marginalized and have a minimal support structure for adequate access to education.

Other ethnic groups affected by trafficking are the Turkish and Slavic-Muslim (Pomaks) minority in Bulgaria. My research shows that Bulgarian-Turkish, and Pomak women are targeted for the increased demands of the Turkish diaspora in Western Europe (mostly Germany and the Netherlands). Kristen Ghodsee reports on the economic decline of the Pomak regions in Bulgaria due to the closing of mines that employed the local population. It is appropriate to refer here again to Sasha Todorova's findings about the close correlation between ethnic belonging and poverty. To the data she offers on the high percentage of impoverished Roma communities, she adds that the poverty risk groups also include "[l]arge families, comprising 8.6 percent of the group, the greater part of whom are ethnic Turks or people of Gypsy descent" (Todorova 1999, 84). This scholar includes one last differentiation by gender in the poverty risk groups: "men comprising 24 percent and women 76 percent" (Todorova 1999, 84). It is the economic necessity of the women, seeking employment and a better life, and the profit that traffickers make that drive the problem.

Lastly, the Mediana Agency writes that 82.4 percent of the participants in the survey believe that it is the responsibility of the state to fight trafficking in human beings. The most alarming of these attitudes indicates a split in the response to trafficking: "It is not bad to be an illegal [term used in the study] worker—it is bad not to get paid and to be turned into a slave. The state should interfere then" (NCCTHB January 2008, 3). The responsibility of the individual to be a law-abiding citizen is missing from the beliefs of the surveyed Bulgarians. This attitude indicates a lack of a developed civic consciousness and a weak democratic society, which, in turn, aid the existence of trafficking. These results suggest the ineffectiveness of anti-trafficking campaigns because they show that myths, stereotypes, and misinformation about trafficking still persist and inform the opinions of many Bulgarians.

Macedonia (Former Yugoslav Republic of Macedonia)

Where the conditions for trafficking and attitudes toward it are concerned, matters are complicated by Yugoslavia's dissolution and the Yugoslav Wars.[1] After the commencement of the wars, the United Nations introduced international sanctions and trade embargoes on the countries involved, in order to hamper their military power and economic viability. In 1991, the UN "imposed a general and complete embargo on all deliveries of weapons and military equipment to Yugoslavia," and in 1992 even more austere sanctions were introduced—full trade embargo and restrictions on the transportation of petroleum, coal, and steel (UN 2002). As a result, smuggling routes became well organized and structured. In the report "Smuggling in Southeast Europe," Marko Hajdinjak states:

---

[1] For the overall conditions of trafficking in Yugoslavia and consequently its independent states, I owe gratitude to Amy Szabo, who wrote an insightful M.A. thesis on the subject.

In the name of the higher goals like protection of national independence and sovereignty, the leaderships of the seceding republics had to set up and arm the newly created republican armies in the only way possible—illegally, by using existing as well as newly established smuggling channels. The party leaders and the high-ranking officers in the Yugoslav army and the secret service largely tolerated these activities and in their turn contributed to the development of a stable smuggling system. (2002, 5)

Smuggling, therefore, became an accepted necessity. Traffickers took advantage of the situation, and their network in the former Yugoslavia utilized the interethnic support that developed during the war. Many of the operations developed to smuggle fuel and weapons across borders are used today to traffic women for forced prostitution:

Trafficking of illegal immigrants through Southeast Europe seems to be organized by the same groups who were previously engaged in the smuggling of weapons and drugs or in "assisting" refugees to reach safety for a price during the war. Similarly, the same routes are being used and the same partners from the other side of the border are involved. This seems to be especially the case in the countries of the former Yugoslavia. (Hajdinjak 2002, 50)

Other sources also confirm the easy collaboration between interethnic organized crime groups. The Institute for War and Peace Reporting (IWPR) points out: "There is no linguistic, religious or any other problem among the criminals" (IWPR 2003).

Images of violence—especially female bodily violations and rapes—became a prevalent part of the media in all former Yugoslav countries. While most war rapes targeted Bosnian Muslim women, ideologues and leaders of all countries manipulated and used gendered imagery, creating a true nationalist phobia (O. Kesić 1999, 187).[2] The gendered nature of the propaganda imagery and the emphasis on rape created attitudes that tolerated violations of human

---

[2] For examples of rapes against different ethnic groups and how they were used in propaganda, see Stiglmayer (1994).

rights and abuse against women. Croatian feminist Vesna Kesić notes that: "women's groups from different parts of former Yugoslavia also reported increases and changes in modes of domestic violence during the war. Women were attacked by their partners with guns and knives and even killed in the streets with hand grenades" (2000, 26). Such were the conditions that influenced the perception of trafficking in Macedonia.

In addition to these factors, which resulted from the legacy of Yugoslavia and its dissolution, ethnic divisions and tensions in Macedonia between Slavic and Christian Orthodox Macedonians and Muslim Albanians (over 30 percent of the population) are also present. During the armed conflict in Macedonia (2000–2001) between the Macedonian Police Forces and the Albanian rebels, a negative attitude emerged towards the Albanians, perceived as the main organizers and perpetuators of human trafficking. This is not to say that there are no Albanian perpetrators and only the stereotypes about them persist. In its 2010–2011 report on the sentences of trafficking perpetrators, the Macedonian organization "Coalition for Fair Trials" indicates that from January to August 2011, 19 Albanians, 14 Macedonians, 1 Roma, 3 Serbs, and 6 people with an unknown ethnic belonging were sentenced to serve time in prison (Gotovski 2010, 9). The ethnic tensions were also fueled by Western media venues, portraying the expansion of the Albanian Mafia into continental Europe, gaining control over the prostitution business in Italy and with an increased control in London. The film *Taken*, discussed in Chapter 4, adds to this construction of Albanians as actors in major criminal organizations. Such international reports and local data about the ethnicity of perpetrators appear to inflate inter-ethnic animosities among the population, as each ethnic group projects blame onto the other. In the reality of organized crime, however, where mainly profit matters, the perpetrators have no problem collaborating with criminals from another ethnic group, as accounts mentioned above demonstrate.

The US annual report on trafficking from 2011 states that trafficking in men, women, and children for both sex and forced labor is an ongoing problem in Macedonia even though sex and labor trafficking have been illegal since 2004, with the minimum penalty for sex trafficking being four years in prison. According to the Macedonian government in 2010, all trafficking victims were domestic citizens and the government is making an effort to combat this crime and human rights violation. It convicted twenty-one sex trafficking offenders in 2010, compared to zero in 2009 and opened a new shelter for trafficking victims in February 2011. Local experts say that the main issue within the Macedonian government seems to lie in identifying trafficked persons (twelve were found in 2010, and only seven in 2009). Macedonia continues its trafficking prevention efforts, using their $550,000 budget from the National Commission to hold awareness campaigns in collaboration with NGOs.

To sum up, the change in the political and economic system in the region, the emergence of independent states, the war and the placement of UN forces (which dramatically increased the demand for trafficked women in the region), alongside linguistic similarities and the cultural interconnectedness and interrelations of various ethnic and religious groups all define the situation of trafficking in the region, former Yugoslavia in general and Macedonia in particular. In her 2004 article, "Regional Sex Trafficking in the Balkans: Transnational Networks in an Enlarged Europe," Nicole Lindstrom quotes data from the International Organization for Migration which claims that 400,000 people are transported through the Balkans into the European Union annually, and that 170,000 more trafficked persons remain in the region (46). An additional report by the European Institute for Crime Prevention and Control states that "more than 80 percent of the victims from South-Eastern Europe (one of the main source areas) end up as prostitutes, and about 10 percent as suppliers of other erotic services" (Lehti 2003, 5).

The United States

Trafficking in people, however, is not only a problem in South Eastern Europe; it has become ever more visible in the United States, too. More and more American neighborhoods—especially in bigger cities— witness trafficking cases.[3] The US government's annual report states

---

[3] For more on the growing problem of trafficking in the US and discussion of its unexpected places and unsuspected perpetrators, see Kevin Bales and Ron Soodalter's *The Slave Next Door*.

that trafficking in men, women, and children is a growing problem in the United States, mainly in areas of forced labor and sex trafficking. Forced labor trafficking has been illegal in the United States since the end of the Civil War, and these laws have been updated and expanded since 2000 to include sex trafficking. Penalties range from five years to life in prison, with a minimum sentence of ten years for sex trafficking offenders. In 2010, the US government convicted 141 individuals in 103 human trafficking cases, the largest number of human trafficking prosecutions in one year. The government is now taking more preventative measures. The United States Department of Justice (DOJ) continues to fund 39 anti-trafficking forces and is currently working on techniques to better gather data and accurate statistics. In addition, DOJ trained more than 24,278 officers on how to spot trafficked persons and how to react to trafficking situations. In 2011, the FBI gave anti-trafficking training to 1,000 new officers, and the US government has increased its aid to a higher number of trafficking victims by increasing funding to NGOs (Gotovski 2010).

The specificity of trafficking in the United States and the overall discourse that surrounds it involves many faith-based organizations, which fund and conduct anti-trafficking activities. While Elizabeth Bernstein records the political impact of evangelical Christians on sex trafficking views, Mark Elliott centers on Christian grass-root groups, reaching out to Congress representatives to exercise pressure and call for Congressional action as well as the activities of the Salvation Army, which Elliott calls the "premier Protestant denominational response to trafficking" (Bernstein 2007; Elliott 2005, 2). Sheldon Zhang contends that some faith-based groups blur the differences between sex trafficking and prostitution, and that discourses surrounding trafficking are shaped more by ideology and moral beliefs than by research or data (2009). Similarly, analyzing US anti-trafficking policies and their discourse under the President George W. Bush administration, Gretchen Soderlund critiques the damaging effects of the "raid-and-rehabilitation" method of abolitionist groups, such as the Christian-based human rights International Justice Mission, which often targets both trafficking and prostitution as equally harmful to human dignity (2005). In her introduction to *Trafficking and Prostitution Reconsidered*, Kemala Kempadoo criticizes the dominant trafficking discourse "as the idea that those who are subject to violence and slavery-like practices are 'victims'" and points out that "the objectifying dimensions of the definition, and its ability to dismiss any conception of will and agency has also been recognized by feminist researchers and theorists" (2011, xxii–xxiii). Overall, moral and religious considerations play a significant role in the perception of and attitudes towards trafficking in the United States.

Recent human rights campaigns against sex trafficking have focused on trafficked persons, treating trafficking as a criminal aberration in an otherwise just economic order. In *Economies of Violence*, Jennifer Suchland critiques these explanations and approaches, and argues that trafficking must be understood not solely as a criminal, gendered, and sexualized phenomenon, but as operating within a global unsafe labor market (2015).

US media (documentary and feature films) increasingly call attention to the problem of trafficking.[4] Under President Barack Obama, the US government intensified its prevention efforts. All these efforts notwithstanding, US citizens tend to be ill informed and continue to harbor myths about trafficking. In 2010, as part of her requirements for graduation with research distinction in psychology in the undergraduate colleges of The Ohio State University, Kristen Silver conducted a socio-psychological survey, "Human Trafficking in the United States: Citizens Empathy & Awareness." Silver describes her methods the following way:

> Participants were 223 undergraduates in introductory psychology courses from The Ohio State University. Participants received no monetary compensation, but did receive course credit for their participation. There were no exclusion criteria, other than that each participant had to be 18 years of age or older. Women comprised 58.3% of the sample and men comprised 41.7%. In terms of age, 21.5% of the sample was 18 years of age, 37.7% was 19 years of age, 17% was 20 years of age, 8.5% was 21 years of age, 4.9% was 22 years of age, 2.2% was 23 years of age, and 8.1% was 24 years of age or older. (2010, 24)

---

[4] Of the 59 films shown at the UN.GIFT film forum in 2008, 27 were either productions or co-productions of the United States.

Furthermore, she specifies the religious and political orientations of the participants, consisting of Catholics (27.8%), non-denominational Christians (23.8%), Protestants (13.5%), and Orthodox Christians (3.1%), agnostics (13%), atheists (4%), Muslims (3.1%), Hindus (2.2%), and Jewish (2.2%). Students were also asked to identify their political orientation: the predominant group claimed to be moderate (39%) with conservatives and liberals forming equal shares of 26.5% (Silver 2010, 25). The design of the study offered four different versions of a vignette with two independent variables: citizenship of sex worker (foreign or domestic) and consensual nature of sexual activity (voluntary or involuntary). The foreign women were described as being from Ukraine because of the high number of trafficked persons from this country. Silver continues describing her design:

> Women involuntarily involved in prostitution were portrayed as trafficked, and women voluntarily involved were portrayed as sex workers. When crossed, these independent variables produced a 2 x 2 design. Responses to various vignettes were used to assess the levels of empathy towards women involved in different forms of sexual activity, as well as collect information on how prosocial inclinations vary based on the circumstances of the woman. (2010, 26)

The following table illustrates the four variables.

Table 2.1: Variables (Silver 2010, 27)

	Voluntary	Involuntary
Foreign	**FV**: Foreign women who migrate internationally to do sex work	**FI**: Foreign women trafficked internationally for sexual exploitation
Domestic	**DV**: Domestic women who migrate internally to do sex work	**DI**: Domestic women trafficked internally for sexual exploitation

I will not present all the findings of the study here, which in general are very illuminating about the ways gender, religion, and political orientation influence beliefs and attitudes toward trafficking, but I will outline some of the most revealing findings and the ones that directly relate to my discussion. As a start, the differences in views, underlined by gender identities, are stunning. Men exhibited lower interpersonal empathy and higher rape myth acceptance; they showed more hostile attitudes towards rape victims and more unclear views towards sex workers; and demonstrated less pro-socially empathetic behavior than women (Silver 2010, 52).

Unlike the conclusions of the Bulgarian Mediana Agency, which claim that Bulgarians recognize trafficking mostly when Bulgarian citizens are involved and disregard the involvement of foreigners, Silver's study shows that American women working as sex workers received the least amount of empathy. Here, however, one should keep in mind that for Bulgarians the willingness to blame trafficked people for their fate increased when the trafficking concerned women in the sex industries. Also, American students distinguished between trafficked women and those who voluntarily engage in sex work. Silver's data implies that there are not only negative attitudes towards women in prostitution, but blaming responses as well.

Furthermore, the condition in the present study that received the least empathy was:

> Domestic/Voluntary—American women working as prostitutes. The data suggest not only negative attitudes toward women in prostitution, but possible blaming reactions and bias concerning Americans trafficked into the sex industry in comparison to trafficked foreign women. (Silver 2010, 54)

What is, however, in my view, culturally specific in the American responses is the assumption that foreign women could be involved in sex work, but Americans should not. Two factors determine these opinions: first, the American myth that the United States is the most prosperous country in the world and its citizens have better opportunities and therefore should not engage in prostitution; and second, the religious beliefs of most respondents, who were more eager to pass moral judgment. Political orientation also contributes to these beliefs. The study proves that liberal students (more likely to be women) believe it is the US government's responsibility to help (Silver 2010, 37).

According to Silver, the participants revealed myths and misconceptions surrounding human trafficking. "Three fourths of the sample (75.7%) falsely believed that human trafficking was equivalent to smuggling" (Silver 2010, 49). These attitudes differ from the ones expressed by Bulgarians, who thought that illegally crossing borders or illegally working abroad does not constitute trafficking, but is a sign of economic stagnation in Bulgaria and people's interest and willingness to seek employment abroad. "When asked if trafficked people could be found in the hospitality industry, 48 percent of American students did not know and only 13.3 percent correctly said yes" (Silver 2010, 50). Similar to the Bulgarian reaction, many Ohio State University students incorrectly viewed human trafficking as a condition requiring physical restraint, bodily harm, or physical force on the part of the trafficker (41.3 percent). Based on the UN definition, coercion or the threat of force is enough to meet legal standards. In addition, 57 percent did not know that there were documented cases of trafficking in Columbus, Ohio—the city where they study (Silver 2010, 49–50).

These brief outlines of the different conditions and attitudes toward trafficked persons and perpetrators in Bulgaria, Macedonia, and the United States suggest that while certain myths about trafficking persist everywhere—perhaps shaped by mediascapes related to trafficking—the political, economic, and cultural backgrounds of individuals and communities also influence their understanding of trafficking, and people in various parts of the world perceive it differently despite its core nature that defines it. In the next two chapters I will shed additional light on these findings. To return to Appadurai, I again evoke his argument that locality is a structure of feeling caused by forms of international activity. While from the brief discussion above it becomes clear that conditions of and attitudes towards trafficking in different regions of the world are affected by international activities, this change does not lead to a common understanding (or literacy) of trafficking. The local comprehension of trafficking is a product of various pressures by still-persistent notions of center and periphery and the resulting tensions of economic and cultural privilege and marginalization, as well as gender and power—all marking the body of local communities.

CHAPTER 2

NGO Prevention Campaigns and Their Audiences

The field of media studies has generated numerous debates about theory, theoretical models, critical approaches, and methodologies, and its history has been shaped by some of these dialogues and disputes. Considering that the object of its investigation—media itself—has evolved so rapidly in the last thirty years, media studies exists in a constant process of reviving its methods and approaches as it responds to new conditions. What is of particular interest to me is audience studies, which developed naturally within the framework of media studies and has mainly been focused on the debate of how and if media "affects" the viewer. The belief that media representations have direct behavioral, psychological, or ideological effects on the spectator has been either denied (Klapper 1969) or further developed (Halloran 1970). More perceptive changes in media scholarship include arguments that center on the agency of the audience, its "gratification" (McQuail 1969), as well as its ability to filter media messages (Morley 1980).

One side of the debate surrounding the influence of media, well represented by television scholar John Fiske, pushed back against cases of media effects or impact. Although Fiske's views have evolved over the years, he always critiqued the alleged power of media to "brainwash" the audience. Even he, however, acknowledges that media hides ideological power. "Television does not 'cause' identifiable effects in individuals; it does, however, work ideologically to promote and prefer certain meanings of the world, to circulate some meanings rather than others, and to serve some social interests better than others" (Fiske 2003, 20).

According to the opposing side, the media environment significantly influences the individual's emotions, attitudes, and behavior. Research from the past decade shows that media contributes to negative emotional conditions, establishes opinions on given social issues, shapes young people's perception of reality, etc. (Bozhinova and Tair 2005, 2008, 2009). Considering the transnational distribution of media products, the problem of the cultural differences of their perception becomes extremely pertinent. Thus, recent media studies scholars have returned to the issues of media power and influence, criticizing a shift towards audience gratification and an active audience. Jenny Kitzenger contends that: "it is vital to maintain concern with media 'impact,' besides being attentive to the ways in which people engage with, criticize, use and resist media messages" (20). In other words, media studies opened a discussion on the effects of media, traveled the road of questioning and debating these "effects," and finally returned again to the "impact" but with consideration of the spectator's agency. This agency, I contend, is shaped by the cultural, economic, political, and gender backgrounds of viewers.

I acknowledge that the debate on the nature of reception and the role of audiences is more complex than the way I summarized it above. Even if Theodor Adorno's "mass deception" and Antonio Gramsci's idea of ideological determinism, or "hegemony," still affect the debate, there are voices (Fiske's, for example), influenced by Michel Foucault, which appeal for a more nuanced critique beyond the accepted "hegemony." Adorno's preoccupation with the logic of the system of consumer capitalism and the reduction of all forms of value to profit captures only some aspects of the study of production. One can argue that such processes motivate the objectification of women's bodies to a certain degree. Gramsci's insistence that the dominant groups must function through negotiations and persuasion and that hegemonic power is achieved through the compliance of subordinated groups, could shed some light on the reception of trafficking films, but it fails in the details and especially in the divergent tastes determined by the different cultural backgrounds of subordinated groups.

Fiske's work reveals the tension between the "hegemonic" model and the Foucauldian concept of decentered and productive power. Although Fiske accepts that the text is still a space for power to create meanings, for him the terms "text" and "audience" should be dissolved and replaced with "textuality" and "intertextuality" of "moments of viewing":

Textuality is realized in the making of sense and the production of pleasure, and central to this process is the inescapable intertextuality of our culture [...]. I wish only to point out that we have now collapsed the distinction between "text" and "audience." The textuality of television, the intertextuality of the process of making sense and pleasure from it, can only occur when people bring their different histories and subjectivities to the viewing process. There is no text, there is no audience, there are only the processes of viewing—that variety of cultural activities that take place in front of the screen which constitute the object of study that I am proposing. (Fiske 1989, 56)

While I concur with the idea that the process of viewing matters, I believe that it is determined by the national, cultural, and economic context (or background) of the viewer, or perhaps related to what Fiske calls "the subjectivity of the viewing process." In other words, my research shows that while production and text matter, audiences' religious and gender identities (just to name these two) shape their responses to media products and influence the creation of meaning. Unlike Fiske, I believe that it is not productive to abandon entirely the concepts of "text" and "audience," and I propose to study them interdependently as I develop my argument on the effectiveness of the trafficking media materials and films. Only a comprehensive analysis of these products—an analysis that explores the tensions between production, text, and audience—provides a constructive critique of the usefulness of media materials in anti-trafficking campaigns. In other words, if the viewer's cultural background alters the connotation of media messages, media products in turn mold the viewer's opinions.

The Macedonian NGO, Otvorena Porta (Open Gate) – LaStrada, based in Skopje and established in 2000, offers comprehensive services to prevent trafficking and aid survivors. In addition to an emergency (SOS) hotline service for violence against women and a shelter for victims of violence and trafficking, Open Gate conducts systematic prevention campaigns. As part of these campaigns, the film *You Are Alive* (2005, Macedonia) is screened to various audiences, followed by a discussion conducted by Open Gate staff members.

In December 2004, Open Gate launched the project "Fighting Human Trafficking in Macedonia," financially supported by the Catholic Relief Services-Macedonia and Caritas-Norway. The project aimed to raise awareness about human trafficking and help its victims. Three different campaigns were held at local and national levels: there were media presentations, fora, educational preventive lectures and workshops; billboards were created in major cities and posters, leaflets, mugs, and pens were distributed. On June 9, 2005, the film *You Are Alive* was shown in the Museum of Contemporary Art in Skopje, as the first Macedonian film addressing the issues of trafficking (Plate 1) (Open Gate 2003–2005 Report 2006, 24). In their 2003–2005 report, they state that in cooperation with the Swedish SIDA, they organized two panel discussions followed by a screening of the film *Lilya 4-ever*. The panels were open to non-governmental and governmental institutions and the participants reached several conclusions about the needs ranging from the protection of victims and the improvement of legislation and coordination between institutions, to the identification of the problem of domestic human trafficking. The film, however, was not part of the discussion (Open Gate 2003–2005 Report 2006, 24).

I spent time in Skopje and visited Open Gate twice: in March 2007 and March 2009. I examined reports and documents related to the organization's prevention campaigns and informed myself about its general work. Open Gate is housed in a relatively small but charming two story building, which looks like a family home, located not far from the city center in a neighborhood with a small open market surrounded by small houses. Approaching the building, one first descends a few steps and walks through a ceramic tile patio with a table and a few chairs. The weather was nice during my stays and we always started with Turkish coffee outside, under an arch formed by grape vines. Only a small plaque above a glass door informs the visitor about the fact that this is Open Gate. Although the NGO's staff members were not the subject of my investigation, I nonetheless wanted to have an accurate understanding of their work and their process in the prevention campaigns and wanted to spend some time with them.[1]

The staff members were very proud of their commissioned film, *You Are Alive*, and their archival documents indicated that they usually organize nine to ten screenings a year of *You Are Alive* to high-school

---

[1] Unlike ethnographers, I did not take notes of my observations. See Clifford Geertz's *The Interpretation of Cultures* (1973). I did, however, take notes when examining their documents.

classes of 20 to 30 students, followed by a discussion of the film. During my second visit in 2009, they confirmed that the campaign was ongoing. Judging from the 2012 and 2014 reports, new video materials have been adopted in their prevention campaigns (Open Gate Reports 2012, 2014).

You Are Alive tells parallel stories of two Macedonian women who are trafficked. They meet in a shelter for survivors and Zhana, who has been there for some time, narrates her life story to the other woman who manages to escape from trafficking at the opening of the film, calls an SOS number, and finds herself in the shelter. Still in shock, the unnamed woman does not speak, so the viewer learns her story through numerous flashbacks. Zhana became pregnant when she was sixteen. She married, but afterward could not bear the restrictions and authoritarian atmosphere of her husband's family home where they lived, so she left and moved back to her mother's with the baby. She was seventeen years old and wanted neither to go back to school nor to live with her mother. Then Perro, who came back from Germany to visit his family, appeared.[2] They fell in love and wanted to go to Germany, but since Zhana had no legal papers, Perro's cousin said he would take her at night to cross the border illegally and meet Perro at a motel. She was forced into prostitution for fifteen years.

The story of the other woman, not identified by name, involved a "loverboy" named Kosta, whom she met at a café. He wrote his telephone number on the back of an S.O.S. help line information card. Her mother had not received her salary for two months and Kosta was so kind to promise her a modeling career and take her to Italy. After some hesitation she agreed, and on the way they stopped at a motel where she was sold to another Macedonian man by the name of Perro. After Kosta left, Perro raped her and other women brought to the motel. The viewer is left to wonder whether this Perro and Zhana's "lover-boy" are the same person. Even if this link between the two women is not clear in the film, their shared experience of trafficking unites them. The film ends with Zhana recording her testimony: "I have a daughter. I have a mother. I don't know where they are. I am alive. I want to live." The

---

[2] It is interesting to note that although the film is in Macedonian, the name "Perro" reminds any viewer with Spanish language knowledge of the word for a dog, which dehumanizes the pimp.

camera cuts to the other woman in the embrace of her mother. They watch Zhana's testimony on television. "I don't know whether it is my fault. I want to hug my daughter and somebody to hug me." The screen blackens and shows the S.O.S number for Open Gate.

Their archival notes indicated that before proceeding with a discussion, they introduce a five-minute break, which I attribute to the possibility of the audience's emotional reaction to the film and the need to contain these emotions and transform them into rational thoughts further generated in the discussion that follows. Three questions frame the discussion: What are the reasons for trafficking? Who is to blame? Where does trafficking happen? Opinions recorded include the following reasons: the family conditions of the two women, the strict environment of Zhana's mother-in-law's house, and economic hardship. Responses to the question of blame include the times in general and the women themselves. An observation was recorded that the blame on women came predominantly from men. It is important to note that there was no mention about viewers who doubted the story. Some express their ignorance about the fact that trafficking happens in Macedonia, similar to the Ohio State students who do not recognize that there is trafficking in Columbus. One ought to also emphasize the response that identifies the economic conditions as a reason. This is significant, and it is noticed among the opinions of Bulgarians as well.

As mentioned, their notes documented that there is a gender divide in some of the reactions, but they do not mention anything about differences in reactions according to the ethnic and religious backgrounds of the audience. At the same time, the Open Gate documents showed that the ethnic breakdown of the victims who sought their assistance in 2006 was the following: Macedonian 5, Albanian 5, Roma, 2, and Turkish 1. Muslim women constituted a majority of victims. The NGO's prevention materials are in both languages, Macedonian and Albanian, but the film is in Macedonian with an option for Albanian subtitles. One can argue that since the native language of the majority of their documented victims is not Macedonian, using the film with subtitles negatively impacts the outcomes of the prevention. Admittedly, the official language of the country is Macedonian but when the identification of viewers with the film's characters is concerned, the mother tongue enhances this identification.

You Are Alive is also used by an NGO in the city of Tetovo, Women's Forum, which pays special attention to interethnic and religious cooperation and activities. In addition to Albanian minorities, Macedonia has a Roma population whose numbers range from the official 2002 census of 2.7 percent to other recent estimates indicating 6.7 percent (ERRC). Open Gate's 2003–2005 report testifies to a special prevention campaign targeting Roma children, conducted with comics and discussions. While the comics have little text, it is in Macedonian (Open Gate Report 2003–2005, 29–30). In this connection, it is important to note that the *Report by the European Roma Rights Centre: Macedonia* (2011) expresses concerns about the disproportionate literacy levels between the Romani communities and their children and the general population (ERRC).

It is reasonable to argue that NGOs working in mixed religious and ethnic communities ought to be more perceptive to the needs of minorities, especially when they are the more vulnerable groups. A film in the viewer's native tongue would perhaps achieve a better level of identification and effectiveness. The same observation can be made about Bulgarian NGOs and their prevention materials. The Bulgarian government data on trafficked people and survivors does not offer any information about their ethnic or religious backgrounds; however, NGOs acknowledge that they work mostly with Romani women and recently with Turkish-Bulgarians.

Similarly to Open Gate, the Bulgarian NGO Asotsiatsiia Animus/ Animus Association, founded in 1994 and based in Sofia, screens films as part of its prevention campaigns mostly in communities identified as "risk groups"—that is, high schools for orphans, predominantly Roma, as well as to policemen and judicial personnel. According to the organization's website, Animus' mission is to "promote healthy communication between people and gender equality in Bulgarian society." With over twenty years of operation, it is one of the largest non-governmental and not-for-profit organizations in Bulgaria and provides a wide range of social services. Anti-trafficking programs are only one part of their work.

At the time of my visit in 2009, they had organized twelve high school screenings and seven with police, court clerks, and judges. Groups consisted usually of ten to fifteen viewers. Unlike the Macedonian NGO, however, Animus Association mainly used *Lilya 4-ever* and occasionally the Bulgarian documentary *Open Your Eyes* (Georgi, 'Dzhaki' Stoev, 2002), sponsored by the International Organization of Migration. In the latter, three Bulgarian women, survivors whom Animus Association assisted, tell their stories.

My visits to Animus were numerous over the years, but I spent more time in 2008 and 2009 (Plate 2). My work there involves regular updates on their trafficking cases and examination of their archives and reports.[3] The NGO is housed in an old neighborhood of mainly two or three story buildings from the first quarter of the twentieth century in downtown Sofia. In a renovated house, which reveals old woodwork and freshly painted walls, Animus has offices for their administrators, therapy rooms for sessions with patients, and a space for their hotline. Their shelter is at a different and undisclosed location. Compared to Open Gate, Animus is a bigger organization, and my visits there were more structured and lacked the casual coffee drinking ritual I experienced in Skopje. It was even difficult to schedule my work there.

According to the staff members who lead the campaigns, *Lilya 4-ever* helps them more than *You Are Alive*, for it stimulates a better discussion and evokes a stronger identification, especially among students who are orphans. It tells the story of not a Bulgarian, but a Russian young woman—a detail that might trigger a distancing effect, which was not mentioned or acknowledged. Lilya is a teenager, residing in a small Russian town that is clearly economically depressed, judging by the living conditions of Lilya and her neighbors. Suffering a series of betrayals from her mother, aunt, teacher, social worker, and a friend, Lilya falls in love with a young Russian, the only person in her life who appears kind and caring. As it happens in these scenarios, he offers to have her join him in Sweden. Without any hesitation and understandably, since the film powerfully conveys her desperation, she decides to go. At the last minute, he comes up with a reason to stay a few days in Russia (his grandmother falls ill) and sends Lilya alone. She will be met by his "boss." In Sweden, she is quickly locked up, raped, and forced into prostitution. After managing to escape, she commits suicide.

---

[3] I studied their documents, took notes, and in a couple of instances asked for clarification when the information provided was unclear to me.

Considering the orphan background of some of the audience, it is not surprising that the staff documented that the high school students expressed strong emotions during the scenes of betrayal and during the rape scenes. This behavior reveals the distress and anxiety that these viewers demonstrate, influenced by the film and the subject of trafficking. The rape also affected adult viewers (court clerks) emotionally. The reaction of men is particularly interesting: staff recorded discomfort among some male viewers, who left the room and did not return. Such responses testify to the processes of denial and a refusal to face the problem, as well as their identification with the male aggressors.

Unlike Open Gate, after some of the school screenings the Bulgarian staff members distributed a questionnaire with two questions: "Did you learn something new about trafficking from *Lilya 4-ever?*" and "Did you believe the story told in the film and why?" I examined a total of 20 answers from students in three different schools, two in the villages of Podem and Bratsigovo and one in Sofia, as all schools educate orphans or economically disadvantaged students. The answers were anonymous. 18 young people learned something new about trafficking and they all believed the story, except one of these 18 who declared that she did not "because she will not let this happen to her." In most cases, the gender of the students becomes obvious from their identification with Lilya, the victim, or from their use of a first person singular feminine form of verbs.[4] At least 15 reactions can be identified as given by women. The answers about the new information that they derived from the film generally revolve around the deception of the "lover-boy." A typical answer states: "Yes, I learned that I can be deceived and sold by the person I care for and believe in." Unsurprisingly, most of the responses to the second prompt address the "verisimilitude" of the trafficking and/or of the cinematic story. They claim: "Because this can happen to any girl"; "The story was very realistic because it can happen to any of us"; "Because this is reality!"; "Because it was totally real"; and "I believed it because all was real and authentic. I know that something so natural can happen to anyone." Only two answers significantly differ with their complete

---

[4] In the Bulgarian language, verb endings in some past tense forms are marked by the gender of the speaker.

lack of engagement. One states: "No comment." And the other: "I don't remember." One can argue that such responses are motivated by the adolescents' either denial of trafficking or their (false) beliefs that they are in full control of their lives.

My analysis of the 18 complete responses reveals the strong identification of the female viewers with the film's trafficking victim and the overall trust in the cultural construct of the trafficking case presented. The use of categorical (but naïve) statements ("Because I will never let this happen to me.") or adjectives and nouns that indicate indignation and increased discomfort ("tragedy," "deceit," "disgust and disgusting but fact" (repeated twice in one answer) mark the students' emotional reaction. While the identification with the character and her situation is undeniable, there was no indication of any questions that the film might have triggered, suggesting a very uncritical and general understanding of the working of cinema and its constructs.

On the back of some of the answers by students in Bratsigovo, the staff members added notes from their discussion. They asked the students to comment on the ending—Lilya's suicide—and to create an alternative ending for her story. Without exception, everyone agreed that the suicide was too sad and difficult for an ending, but, interestingly, when they began to imagine different endings, they were all equally tragic. Some proposed that police discovered Lilya and took her to a hospital, where she passed away. Others imagined her becoming a prostitute and again she died of diseases. Although they exhibited desire for some optimistic solutions to Lilya's destiny in particular and the trafficking situation in general, they remained grounded in reality. This reaction intensifies the critique of Western film productions, which tend to present a more or less happy ending to trafficking cases, such as in the films *Human Trafficking* and *Taken*. The orphaned students' background and the conditions that define their existence undoubtedly motivate a more realistic or pessimistic view of trafficking. Although in the past five years, the Bulgarian state has made concerted efforts to cultivate the practice of foster homes, it still places orphans in state homes and provides care and education until they finish high school and turn eighteen. After that, these young people are left to making a living and providing for themselves without any support. They all know their situation and are rather terrified at the prospects of making a life for themselves. Under these circumstances, their pessimistic reaction to Lilya's destiny can be interpreted as fear of their own future.

Animus staff members recorded another memorable discussion at the high school for orphans in Sofia, an event they made sure I examined. The viewers were both young men and women. When the discussion addressed the reasons for trafficking in general and in the film in particular, all the male students vehemently blamed Lilya and refused to recognize that the young man with whom she fell in love is in fact a "loverboy." They even claimed that it was unclear from the film whether he really traffics her or whether it was his "boss" who abused her and took advantage of the situation. Sensing the male students' aggression, the staff members decided to divide the viewers into prosecutors and defenders and give them the option to join either team. All the male students joined the prosecutor's team and all young women became Lilya's defenders. The young men were clearly winning the debate by being aggressive and by calling Lilya a "whore" and "bitch." Unlike the adult male viewers, who expressed discomfort and left the screening, these young men's identification with the perpetrators in the film created an opposite reaction: they openly blamed the victim. The female students, on the other hand, identifying with Lilya, felt attacked and helpless. Their distress prevented them from constructing a coherent and effective defense of the victim. They were so powerless that at the end, the leader of the male group decided to switch teams and join the defenders. In addition to restoring some balance in the discussion, this reaction shows these young people's awareness of the power of rhetoric, but also the deep-seated gender attitudes and behavior in these high schools.[5]

These activities in the prevention campaign, using *Lilya 4-ever*, clearly speak of the importance of the gender identification of viewers and the ways they relate to the characters in the film. The above examples suggest that female students emotionally connect to Lilya's victimization and male viewers exhibit other reactions. Whether the male response is a defensive reaction in which the young men identify with the male aggressors in the film and want to shake off their guilt by

---

[5] For the reconstruction of this discussion, I asked the staff for clarification and details because their notes were very brief.

blaming the victim is speculative, but it is important to emphasize that both the Macedonian social workers and the Bulgarian staff members documented varying audience reaction based on gender identities.

In the summer of 2012, aided by an Ohio State University Merhson Center for International Security grant, my work with Bulgarian NGOs continued, and I visited several Bulgarian public organizations that provide anti-trafficking programs and work with minorities. In a small village, 6 kilometers (4 miles) from Veliko Turnovo, a social club (Open Your Eyes: There are People Who Can Help You) was established seven years prior, initially funded by a European grant and at that time supported by the county of Veliko Turnovo. A pedagogue is employed to provide extra-curricular activities for about 50 middle and high school students in the local community.[6] The programs range from interactive lessons, designed to actively involve the students through games and performances, which focus on socially relevant topics such as ecology, drug abuse, volunteer work in the village's Club of Senior Citizens, etc. An important part of these programs is anti-trafficking awareness. Under the guidance of the pedagogue, the students watched *Human Trafficking* and discussed it, dramatized a trafficking situation, created visual materials, and even presented their work at the US Embassy in Sofia invited by Ambassador John Beyrle.

Located in the Culture House on the village square (Plate 3), the social club Open Your Eyes operates in a large hall, equipped with three computers and fitness stations. The enthusiasm and dedication of the pedagogue became immediately apparent when she wanted to show me all of the programs, lesson plans, and visual materials that the students created themselves. Although the pedagogue, an energetic woman in her thirties, wanted to tell me all about the community center's seven-year history, I was interested mostly in how it uses media in the prevention of trafficking and how it works with minorities. She showed me media materials (clips and one documentary) from more specialized anti-trafficking NGOs and also her notes on the screening and discussion of the US/Canada production *Human Trafficking*. Her lesson plan stated that this film was most appealing because it showed

---

[6] In 2011, another group of young people (age 18 to 35) joined the club.

"how trafficking unfolds in a real-life situation." In *Human Trafficking*, after the deaths of three young Eastern European prostitutes, a Russian-American NYPD agent (played by Mira Sorvino) unravels the stories of trafficked women and children. In the end, the criminal ring is destroyed by US forces and the trafficking victims are freed. The pedagogue's summary of the activity indicated that students were shocked to learn that one can be trafficked so easily and in so many different ways. No doubt, the film proffers an accurate representation of recruitment and enslavement into trafficking, but it also presents a happy ending, in which "good" prevails over "evil," a highly questionable scenario in trafficking that the orphaned high school students in Animus lead discussion of *Lilya 4-ever* hoped for but denied. In addition, *Human Trafficking* objectifies women and perpetuates certain stereotypes, as it will become clear later in the book. One should not doubt the good design and execution of the activity and the fact that the film provided a forum for a lively discussion on the subject of trafficking, but one still has to ask questions about all aspects of these films and their latent messages.

The region of the village of Resen has minorities of both Turkish and Roma students. When I asked the pedagogue whether they participate in the club, she confirmed with her typical enthusiasm and quickly added that she does not separate her students according to their ethnic or religious background, and that her most active student is a Turkish girl. I did not notice any preventive materials in Turkish or Roma languages, but I did read in her monthly program of events that they spent a couple of weeks learning about and celebrating the values of the Christian family. It appeared to me that there was no recognition that Muslim students might feel alienated. Despite the supposition that some of this club's activities might not produce the desired effect, the overall effort and work in this local community to engage students with socially important matters is commendable (Plates 4 and 5).

My work with these three NGOs adds a layer of complexity to the way films are utilized in prevention campaigns and are perceived by audiences, highlighting shortcomings in their selection and use relevant to the ethnic and religious belonging of the target viewers. More importantly, however, my analysis shows that gender identities persistently determine the viewer's perception of the trafficked women and the male perpetrators. While the previous chapter outlines some basic differences in the political, economic, and cultural backgrounds of individuals and communities, which impact their general attitudes towards trafficking, this chapter focuses on specific responses to trafficking films and reveals a deep gender divide in people's reactions. My examination of prevention campaigns also indicates that while some NGOs use their own commissioned media materials and others utilize well-circulated Western feature films, there is certainly a need for a more critical selection of these materials, considering the ethnic and linguistic background of their target audience. I concede that it is difficult to follow this suggestion due to complexities of funding and recourses, but I still insist that more thought should be invested in the use of media.

CHAPTER 3

Cross-cultural Discussion of Attitudes toward Trafficking

Media venues are some of the main source of information about trafficking in people. The information dispersed through media among other factors shapes individual and social attitudes towards trafficking—negative or positive—and, some argue, people's emotional and behavioral conditions. In this context, so-called "information behavior" is extremely important (Wilson 2000). The information behavior is characterized as the individual's comprehensive behavior in relation to the sources and channels of information: on the one hand, a person's active and passive search, and, on the other, their use of information.

In the following pages, I present a study that a team of scholars, including myself and two social psychologists from the Bulgarian Academy of Sciences, Roumiana Bozhinova and Ergyul Tair, conducted.[1] Our objectives were:

- To examine the attitudes of young people in the US and Bulgaria towards human trafficking, particularly the overall assessment of the phenomenon and its reasons, the emotional reaction and behavioral readiness to act in order to prevent and combat the problem.

---

[1] A shorter version of this study was previously published as "Knowledge and Attitudes towards Trafficking in People: Cross-Cultural Differences" (R. Bozhinova, E. Tair, and Y. Hashamova). *Bulgarian Journal of Psychology* 1.4 (2010): 41–51.

- To study the level of information (knowledge) the two groups of young people have about trafficking.
- To explore the correlation between the level of information and the attitudes the two groups show.

We expected that there were cross-cultural differences in the attitudes towards major contemporary social problems, and in particular towards trafficking in people. These differences were reflected in the cognitive, emotional, and behavioral components of the attitudes. We also presumed that these differences are connected to the level of information young people have in each country. While in the previous two chapters, I argued that local identity markers such as national, cultural, and gender identities affect people's attitudes towards trafficking, part of this study probes the question as to whether the information horizon (or "behavior," to use Wilson's term) influences people's responses and readiness to become involved with anti-trafficking projects. This is an important aspect of the double bind relationship between viewers and their cultural backgrounds, which impact their beliefs about trafficking on the one hand, and the information shaping their perceptions, on the other.

METHOD

The study surveyed a total of 170 students: 104 Bulgarian (from Sofia and Plovdiv Universities) and 66 American (from Ohio State University). The sample is gender balanced (49.4% males and 50.6% females). In the American sample, the males comprise 66% and the females 34%. In the Bulgarian sample, 61.5% are female and 38.5% are male. The age ranges between 18 and 46, with the average age being 21 (M=21.3). The level of information about and attitudes towards trafficking in people was analyzed through a survey designed for this particular study. The survey consists of seventeen items regarding the subject matter and demographic data. The students were surveyed at the beginning of class sessions.

DESIGN

Both American and Bulgarian students were asked to indicate their agreement with the following 17 statements. The study also asked them to identify the level of their knowledge on the subject, their age, and gender (see Table 3.1 below).

Table 3.1: Survey of Knowledge of Human Trafficking

1 Strongly disagree
2 Somewhat disagree
3 Somewhat agree
4 Strongly agree

	Statements	Scale			
1	Cases of trafficking in people are often reported in the U.S. media	1	2	3	4
2	Many people are abducted and forced to work abroad	1	2	3	4
3	Trafficking in people is inevitable in today's global world	1	2	3	4
4	Trafficking in people has a series of positive aspects	1	2	3	4
5	I think that everyone should be prepared to defend him/herself from trafficking	1	2	3	4
6	I would like to get involved in an anti-trafficking organization	1	2	3	4
7	Trafficking in people is a business matter	1	2	3	4
8	People have to openly protest against trafficking	1	2	3	4
9	Anyone can become a victim of trafficking	1	2	3	4
10	People are naïve and perpetuate the problem of trafficking	1	2	3	4
11	Society as a whole is responsible for the phenomenon of trafficking	1	2	3	4
12	Trafficking is an opportunity for some people to escape from poverty in their own country	1	2	3	4
13	Usually people are willingly trafficked	1	2	3	4
14	Trafficking in people is not a problem that deserves attention	1	2	3	4

Statements	Scale			
15	The life of trafficked people is horrible	1	2	3	4
16	Perpetrators of trafficking and pimps are the core of the problem	1	2	3	4
17	Trafficking is one of the worst things that can happen to people	1	2	3	4
18	About trafficking in people: 1 – I know nothing 2 – I know very little 3 – I know the basics 4 – I know a lot You are: Male / Female Age:				

After the participants marked their answers, the Bulgarian documentary *Open Your Eyes* was screened and students were asked to comment on it, using four to five words as well as four sentences. It is important for this analysis to note that the group of Bulgarian students does not include Film Studies majors, whereas some of the American students majored in Film Studies.

The film incorporates the testimonies of three survivors of trafficking. They give brief information about their backgrounds and narrate the ways they were recruited, their experiences in traffic, and their escapes. Wendy Hesford has criticized the film, like many other such films, because it identifies "women as passive and naïve victims lured and tricked into sex work and therefore in need of rescue…" (2005, 147). In my class discussion with Ohio State University students, only one female student recognized the framing of these survivors as passive victims because of the male figure, a Bulgarian rock star, who ends the film, appealing to "girls [sic]" to be careful. Bulgarian students did not respond to this gender hierarchy. They did not notice any weaknesses in the aesthetics either or at least did not comment on them. My Film Studies students, however, elaborated at length on the "inadequate" montage, which combined the women's sober and emotional testimonies with scenes from streets in Western Europe (most likely Amsterdam), which display sex workers at shop windows. The differences in the observations of these groups of students point to the educational background as a factor in the perception of media products. This finding adds to my previous argument that identity factors (national, cultural, and gender) impact attitudes towards trafficking. Educational background becomes another important marker that ought to be considered when prevention campaigns using media materials are organized.

RESULTS AND DISCUSSION

The attitudes are examined in the context of the overall assessment and reasons, emotional and behavioral readiness to act in order to prevent trafficking. The results, revealing the assessment and the understanding for the underlying reasons, display important tendencies. According to our data analysis, the two groups (American and Bulgarian) share the opinion that trafficking is "inevitable" in today's global world. At the same time, most of the students view trafficking as a danger to everyone, but this fear is most pronounced among the Bulgarians ($t=5.34$; $p=.000$). The relatively similar assessment of trafficking as inevitable and a serious danger reveals the social significance of the problem to all individuals surveyed regardless of their nationalities. The difference in the perception of trafficking as dangerous (higher in the Bulgarian case) can be explained by the knowledge that Bulgaria is more affected by trafficking as a donor country and the higher risks of being trafficked that Bulgarians face.

In contrast, the data also show a common perception that trafficking has "positive" implications. This is a surprising finding. The statement "Trafficking in people has a series of positive aspects" was placed mostly to check the respondents' attentiveness, as we expected mostly negative answers, but the results varied. The difference is well illustrated through the frequency analysis (Figures 3.1a and 3.1b). It is also interesting to note that the two groups consider trafficking as an "economic opportunity" for some to escape poverty. Obviously, in the minds of both groups of students, the concept of trafficking and its nature are ambiguous and confusing. One can argue that smuggling and trafficking overlap for these groups, who perceive undocumented labor migration similar or identical to trafficking. Perhaps the idea of voluntary sex work also plays a role in this confusion. Considerably more Bulgarians express this view (Figure 3.1b). This divergence likely results from the nature of trafficking in Bulgaria (donor country) and the United States (destination country) and the way these two communities interpret trafficking.

Figure 3.1a: Trafficking has Positive Implications

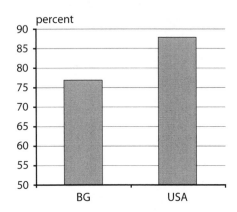

Figure 3.1b: Trafficking as an Opportunity to Escape from Poverty in Own Country

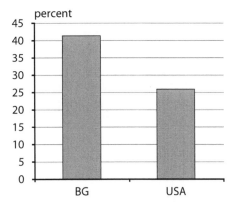

Furthermore, our analysis points to a gripping perception of the ultimate reasons for the existence of trafficking in today's global world.
First, both groups believe that the individual alone is responsible
for his or her involvement in trafficking. The second most frequent
response blames the "naïveté" of certain people, and the third, the
perpetrators. This finding reveals a common response among people
of various communities, who tend to cast blame on the victim rather
than the perpetrator or the economic conditions. The same reactions
are noticed among the viewers of the Balkan NGOs' prevention campaigns discussed earlier. A substantial divergence can be noticed in the

understanding of two factors for trafficking: 1) trafficking as a "business" matter, and 2) the role of society as a whole. Bulgarians place an emphasis on the role of "business with people" (36%) and Americans on the responsibility of society (50%) (Figure 3.2). This discrepancy can be viewed in the light of the differences in information about trafficking dispersed in the two countries.

For example, from October 2008 to October 2009, several months before and after this study was conducted, BTV, the most watched TV network in Bulgaria, aired fifteen reports related to human trafficking. Six of them address local or international criminal trafficking rings more generally, as some indicate changes in the Bulgarian law or quote statements of politicians. More interestingly, nine of these reports inform about arrests of individuals or criminal rings accused of a series of crimes, including money laundering, trafficking, prostitution, and racketeering. Four of these nine spell out the amounts of profit and offer numbers that range from 50,000 euros to 1,000,000,000 euros. None focus on the circumstances of the trafficked people, their economic conditions, or their human rights violations. With such media coverage that centers on the profitable aspect of the crime rather than on its human rights dimensions, for instance, it is unsurprising why Bulgarian students viewed human trafficking as "business with people."

Figure 3.2: Reasons for the Existence of Trafficking in Today's Global World

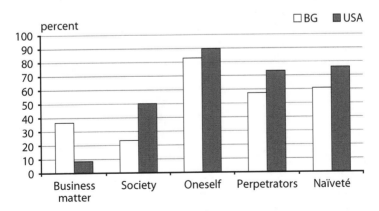

The emotional component of the attitudes also reveals the presence and/or absence of cross-cultural differences. Our data show that both groups react emotionally to the problem. This tendency, however, is better expressed among the American students. A significantly larger percentage of them believe that "the life of trafficked people is horrible" (t=2.67; p=.008). In a similar manner, most of them think that "trafficking is one of the worst things that can happen to people" (t=2.02; p=.05). This variant can be interpreted with the fact that there is a tendency in Bulgaria to play down the negative impact of trafficking and to look at it as an "economic opportunity," as the media reports mentioned above indicate.

The behavioral readiness to act is the third aspect of the attitudes that our study investigates. The readiness to take a stand against trafficking in people appears to be similar between the two groups (Figure 3.3). Both Bulgarian and American young people express eagerness to participate in organizations combatting trafficking. Significant variance can be noted in the views whether the individual alone ought to protect him- or herself from trafficking, an opinion that appears to be more strongly expressed by the American students (t=2.79; p=.006). This result most likely reflects overall social and cultural constructions, which, in the United States, value and cultivate the power of the individual to deal with all situations in life.

Figure 3.3: The Behavioral Readiness to Act among Bulgarian and American Students

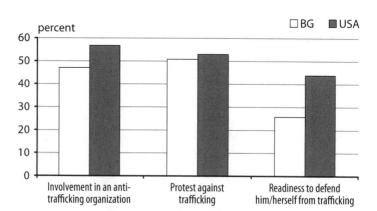

Following our objectives, the study also examines the level of information (knowledge) about trafficking in the two groups (Bulgarian and American). As the results in Figure 3.4 show, the Bulgarian students are better informed about trafficking. The most visible difference emerges in the basic knowledge the two groups have about trafficking: 15% percent more Bulgarian (than American) students define themselves as well-informed. There is also a difference in the number of people who define themselves as knowing a lot or knowing nothing. More American (than Bulgarian) students place themselves in these two extreme positions.

Figure 3.4: The Level of Information about Trafficking Between Two Groups

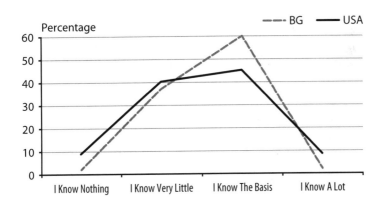

The study proves our hypothesis that the level of information affects attitudes towards trafficking. This conclusion emerges from the two groups regardless of their nationality. In addition, students who are more informed reveal a deeper and more complex view on the problem. For these people (more than for the less-informed), trafficking requires special attention (t=2.02; p=.046), because the problem is a fact and many people are forced to work outside their countries (t=3.05; p=.003). Along with the negative aspects of trafficking, these (more informed) students also see "positive elements" (t=2.07; p=.040), for example cheap labor for the destination country. Here, it is important to stress that the positive element is perceived in economic, not moral terms, although one can argue that they are interwoven. The people who claim to be more knowledgeable about trafficking attribute a larger role to the individual for his or her involvement in trafficking (t=2.10; p=.038), an opinion that directly speaks to the type of information they receive or the accuracy of their knowledge.

Consequently, we note that the better informed students are more ready and eager to participate in anti-trafficking organizations (t=3.34; p=.001) and to openly protest against trafficking (t=2.02; p=.045). These results are important for the study of cross-cultural differences, since the Bulgarian sample of students appear better informed than the American.

The specificity of the link between the level of information and the attitudes towards trafficking is determined with the assistance of correlation analysis. Our results show that an increase in the level of information among Bulgarians is directly related to the understanding that many people are kidnapped and enslaved abroad (r=.20; p=.05), and also to the better expressed emotional assessment that trafficking is one of the worst things that can happen to people (r=.20; p=.05). It is significant to note that the increased informational level among Bulgarians leads to the (mis)perception of the "positive aspects" of trafficking (r=.28; p=.001). And last, the increased information also triggers increased readiness to combat trafficking (r=.20; p=.05). The nature of the information about trafficking and the level of the Bulgarian students' informational horizon undoubtedly play a role in their position regarding the "positive aspects" of trafficking. As outlined above, during the studied year (10/2008–10/2009), the Bulgarian TV network, BTV, focused primarily on the profitable side of trafficking and completely ignored the human rights violations and the social conditions of victims, the difficulties of trafficked persons to escape, survive, and reintegrate in society, etc. Such tendencies create a one-sided picture of this crime and therefore the media's contribution to accurately presenting trafficking is questionable.

The increased level of information on trafficking among the American students is mainly connected with the confirmation of the belief that the number of trafficked people forced to work abroad is very high (r=.27; p=.001). The positive correlation between the level of information and the readiness to get involved in anti-trafficking organizations reveals another significant result (r=.50; p=.000). These cross-cultural differences cannot be interpreted unilaterally. They can be attributed to the degree of media coverage of trafficking and its overall stand on trafficking, cultural and national differences, and religious and political orientations, which we did not test. It is important to note here that the study does not examine the precision and accuracy of the information the students claim to have, but registers only the correlation between it and attitudes.

Some of the most important findings of the study include the cross-cultural differences in attitudes towards trafficking. American students hold a more general (abstract) view of the "positive aspects" of trafficking, while Bulgarians connect the "positive side" to concrete economic opportunities or profit for the criminals as well as escape from poverty and seeking employment for the victims. The reasons for trafficking are also perceived differently: Americans believe that the whole society is responsible for it, while Bulgarians ascribe it to "business with people"—that is, to its economic side and the profit-making operation.

The findings that the level of information influences the attitudes towards trafficking, and that students who are more informed view trafficking in a more complex manner and declare a higher level of readiness to get involved in anti-trafficking organizations, are most important for my argument. As I contend, although all trafficking films and media products are created by socially engaged filmmakers, often their films present misleading and inaccurate information about trafficking and negatively affect the information level of the audience. The data suggest that the Bulgarian media covers the phenomenon more widely than the American media, centering on its profitability. At the same time, not only the quantity but also the quality of information (the substance and format) and how it is perceived and interpreted by young people can affect the way information relates to attitudes. These conclusions only reconfirm that further studies are required for a deeper and more comprehensive investigation into the influence of media on the attitudes towards trafficking.

This study pursues the evidence that cultural, historical, and political conditions of certain communities influence people's opinions on trafficking, and it pairs this evidence with the examination of general attitudes towards trafficking among different groups as they intersect with media impact and viewers' responses to media messages about trafficking. My analysis reveals that while certain cultural (political, gender, and religious) identifications of viewers influence their attitudes towards trafficking, film and media messages and information also shape viewers' opinions, and these two factors—background and media environment—interact in a complex way and affect the prosocial position of viewers.

Separate social studies on attitudes toward trafficking in Bulgaria and the United States and my observations on viewers' responses to trafficking films suggest that there are two important elements to the perception of trafficking: 1) cultural and national conditions influence people's attitudes, while media also shapes opinions and often perpetuates myths about trafficking; and 2) gender identifications transcend different cultural backgrounds, as in all examined groups, the studies reveal (mostly male) blaming attitudes towards trafficked women. These findings speak yet again to the importance of media coverage and most specifically of accurate and objective media coverage without perpetual myth creation or one-sided information. With these thoughts in mind, in the next chapters I will analyze a number of feature films and documentaries, and explore how and why media products affect the viewer's understanding of trafficking.

PART TWO

The Representation

CHAPTER 4

Western Feature Films and Media

Undoubtedly, in addition to artistic abilities and filmmakers' backgrounds and understanding of marketing and audiences, capital and profit influence the final media or cinematic product. My content analysis of media materials and films reveals that Western, East European, and co-productions all construct stereotypes of trafficking victims and perpetrators, or as Richard Dyer puts it: "[They] make visible the invisible, so that there is no danger of it creeping up on us unawares" (2004, 250). Significantly, however, the stereotypes that these films portray differ depending on their production origins and agenda. In his essay "The Role of Stereotypes," Dyer summarizes and expands on the definition of the concept coined by Walter Lippmann. Dyer reiterates Lippmann's four major elements in the construction of stereotypes: "(i) an ordering process, (ii) a 'short cut,' (iii) referring to 'the world,' and (iv) expressing 'our' values and beliefs" (Dyer 2004, 246). But what matters for Dyer is not only the construction and its process, but who controls it:

> Throughout, I move between the more sociological concern of Lippmann (how stereotypes function in social thought) and the specific aesthetic concerns (how stereotypes function in fictions) that must also be introduced into any consideration of media representations. The position behind all these considerations is that it is not stereotypes, as an aspect of human thought and representation, that are wrong, but who controls and defines them, what interests they serve. (2004, 246)

Driven by this same objective, in this chapter I not only deconstruct stereotypes but also disclose the conscious or unconscious interests they serve. Whereas in *Moving People, Moving Images*, William Brown, Dina Iordanova, and Leshu Torchin dedicate a large part of the argument to the liminal nature of trafficking and the impossibility (or difficulties) of its representation (considering the impossibility of representing traumatic experiences), I explore the question differently, namely, I ask not about the authenticity of the representation of the "invisible" trafficking victims, but about who controls these representations and whether they are effective. After expansive media awareness campaigns (outlined in the introduction), the production of numerous feature films with considerable box office success, and the institutionalization of dozens of anti-trafficking academic centers in the United States and NGOs both here and in Europe, the visibility/invisibility issue has achieved new dimensions. Scholarship has also developed significantly on the issue of trauma and its representation, which will be addressed in the last chapter. What remains important is how awareness campaigns structure and produce messages about trafficking and whose interests they serve. Anthropologist Carole S. Vance convincingly exposes the narrative structure of anti-trafficking videos based on the axis of good and evil, and terms them "melomentaries." She contends that although the subject matter of such analysis might appear appropriate for cultural studies, it has serious policy implications, too. Vance writes:

> Deconstructing the narrative devices of anti-trafficking videos would seem best done in journals of cultural criticism, except for the fact that these representations have serious consequences for law and policy, as well as for the public that cares about human rights issues. Representations frame the problem, identify causes, and promote interventions and solutions, though often the analytic frame is submerged or hidden by the dramatic, colorful details and the seeming authenticity of the real (especially in the form of video). As a result, these narratives are inadequately scrutinized for the ways in which their underlying analyses seek to explain trafficking. Compellingly crafted, anti-trafficking videos mobilize emotional and urgent support for interventions on the part of nongovernmental organizations (NGOs), states, and

international organizations alike. But what interventions? For what purpose? For which people in what situations? (2012, 201)

Vance's questions underline a critical inquiry into the production of anti-trafficking media and films and they latently permeate my discussion of the selected feature films and documentaries.

Feature Films: The Western World – Powerful and (Self)Critical

As mentioned in the introduction, trafficking in people clearly exemplifies how the West and Eastern Europe have occupied the two sides of Karl Marx's formula of supply and demand, in which human bodies and labor are in demand and insolvent and marginalized communities in Eastern Europe supply them.[1] Films such as *Human Trafficking*, *Sex Traffic*, *The Whistleblower*, and *Eastern Promises*, for example, all portray the supply and demand sides of trafficking. With a varied degree of critique, the West is portrayed as a critical force of demand but also (and perhaps paradoxically) of superior morality and power, which in most cases prevails in the battle against trafficking.

Considering the tragedy of the trafficked persons and the pursuit of the criminals depicted, the genre of *Human Trafficking* can be defined as a criminal drama (police investigation). The director Christian Duguay works mostly for television and has received several Primetime Emmys. For *Human Trafficking* he was awarded the Directors Guild of Canada: Outstanding Direction—Television Miniseries and a Gemini Award: Best Dramatic Miniseries. In the United States, the Lifetime channel's mission to target female viewers in a way dictated the choice of genre for *Human Trafficking* as a criminal drama with a conflict between good and evil and with a happy ending brought to the viewer by a strong woman. In a 1994 issue of *Camera Obscura*, Jackie Byars and Eileen R. Meehan define the network's genre policies in the following way: "Lifetime is committed to the notion that upscale audiences of working women,

---

[1] For more on the reasons and routs of trafficking for sexual exploitation, see Kligman and Limoncelli (2005).

homemakers, and men will watch melodramas in which strong women overcome adversity, particularly if that triumphant struggle involves the love of a good man" (39). Admittedly, in *Human Trafficking* Lifetime moves away from melodrama but unfailingly creates the image of an independent and strong-willed professional woman who, nonetheless, needs the approval and support of her male supervisor to succeed.

Human Trafficking interweaves the stories of three trafficked persons: a young Czech woman, a sixteen-year-old girl from Ukraine, and a twelve-year-old American girl kidnapped in Manila. The powerful international network of sex traffickers, led by a Russian criminal boss, Sergei Karpovich (Robert Carlyle), is responsible for their abuse and violation. The main action unfolds in New York City, where after the deaths of three Eastern European women, the viewer meets the Russian-American New York Police Department (NYPD) agent Kate Morozov (Mira Sorvino). Gaining permission from the Immigration and Customs Enforcement Chief Bill Meehan (Donald Sutherland), she leads the investigation of these cases.

The film opens with a disturbing scene, in which a young Russian girl, shown to the viewer through long takes of her legs, climbs the stairs of a dilapidated hotel (presumably renting rooms by the hour). A Russian thug (recognized as such when he speaks Russian, although with an American accent) follows her and forces her into the room of an obese American client. The man pays for her and begins to expose himself when the girl, terrified, jumps out of the window. Morozov, who appears at the scene, is concerned because this is the third suicide of an East European woman in two months. From this first scene, the viewer immediately recognizes the basic nature of trafficking and the players in this film: the United States is the destination country, with its clients who continuously demand sexual services; Russian girls are trafficked by Russian criminals; and a NYPD agent sets a goal to dismantle the criminal organization.

The viewer observes four different ways through which women are trafficked in the film. A "loverboy" promises a bright future to a Czech single mother, Helena, who bartends but still cannot make ends meet.[2]

---

[2] For a well-researched and nuanced account of Russian women who, because of the lackluster conditions in Russia and limited life opportunities, seek US

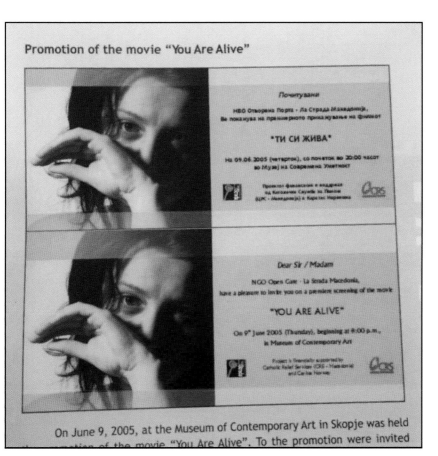

Open Gate's report on the premiere of *You Are Alive*

Author photographed outside of Animus Association

Culture House (village Resen)

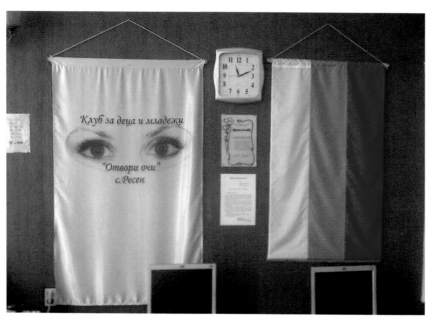

Flag of the Social Club Open Your Eyes made by the students in village Resen

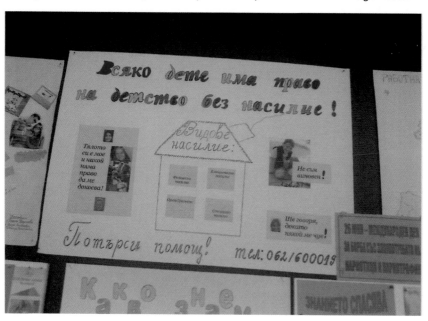

Poster displayed at Open Your Eyes

Still from the opening of the second part of *Human Trafficking*

Kate and Bill discuss the operation in front of the symbol for
US Homeland Security (*Human Trafficking*)

Pimp kills one of the trafficked women (*Sex Traffic*)

Pimp beats a trafficked woman (*Sex Traffic*)

Kernwell's leaders report on addressing the corruption (*Sex Traffic*)

Bosnian man warns perpetrators about upcoming raid (*Whistleblower*)

Local policeman hesitant to assist Bolkovac (*Whistleblower*)

Helena's basement room (*Human Trafficking*)

Nadia's apartment, shared with her father (*Human Trafficking*)

Abandoned by her mother, Lilya is approached by a stray dog (*Lilya 4-ever*)

He takes her to Vienna, where she is sold and forced to provide sexual services. A Kiev teenager, Nadia, is lured by a modeling agency and her dream of a prosperous life in the West turns into a nightmare of trafficking with twelve clients per day. Annie, a twelve-year old American, is snatched from an open market in Manila. A Filipino father, unable to feed his family, sells his daughter, who appears to be the same age as Annie. While these stories unfold and intersect, the viewer learns not only more details about the abuse and violation of these young women, who are deprived of any human rights and treated as commodities to make profit to their "owners," but also about the mechanisms of how they are kept in constant fear for their lives and the lives of their loved ones back home. The film depicts the traffickers' techniques of physical violence and psychological blackmail and abuse, which break the trafficked women's will and identity, guaranteeing that they strictly follow orders.

Although Duguay accurately portrays the horrific nature of trafficking, he also creates a global dichotomy. With the happy ending, in which Morozov successfully eliminates the Russian criminal boss Karpovich, breaks the whole criminal ring, and saves all of the trafficked girls (except Helena, who is killed), the film leaves the viewer with an impression of the power of the United States and its commitment to and success in combatting this global threat. Although Americans are implicated as clients of the trafficked women in New York and also in Manila, the overall portrayal of the United States is built through that of the security forces, and particularly of Kate Morozov and the immigration and customs official Bill Meehan, the dedicated and determined professionals and caring human beings. The casting of Mira Sorvino and Donald Sutherland in these two roles significantly contributes to their dominance in the story and on the screen. Their charismatic acting adds to the perception of skilled and devoted American officers, as a symbol of the United States' overall role in the fight against trafficking.

The second part of the film opens with the title "New York" (Plate 6). New York is introduced to the viewer through a powerful

---

husbands via Internet listings, see Ericka Johnson's *Dreaming of a Mail-Order Husband.*

aerial shot of the city's skyscrapers with all their might. After this panoramic shot, the camera zooms down and shows two FBI agents in a car with surveillance equipment. The next scene reveals Karpovich's mansion and his paranoid fear of being detected. Soon after this, Morozov and Meehan discuss the operation in the Homeland Security quarters and Kate, devastated that Helena was killed on her watch, receives the order to infiltrate the Russian criminal ring, undercover as one of the trafficked East European women. Her sadness and guilt are quickly replaced by determination after she hears: "You have the guts. Go get the bad guys!" When Kate is being told this, she and Bill Meehan are positioned in front of the sign for US Homeland Security, alluding to the US power and its security agencies (Plate 7). The cliché phrase "Go get the bad guys!" adds to the stereotype of the United States as the righteous global police with the moral obligation to restore justice, but it also weakens the credibility of the trafficking experience portrayed in the film. The banal dialogue, paired with the black-and-white depiction of the criminals—all Russians— and the combatting force and rescuers—all Americans—furthers the stereotypes created in the film. While these stereotypes function as an ordering process (to echo Dyer) of "us-good" and "they-bad," it is always pertinent to ask what purpose they serve. In this binary presentation of the world, the American clients, and who are also "bad guys" and who make this business so profitable, escape the attention of the filmmakers.

In this film, Kate leads the narrative and not only destroys the Russian criminal ring but also saves the East European victims, thus functioning as a protector of the vulnerable and the marginalized. Despite the personal anti-trafficking efforts of Mira Sorvino, who was an ambassador for Amnesty International's Stop Violence Against Women program and, no doubt, the good intentions of the filmmakers, *Human Trafficking* does not avoid reinforcing old stereotypes about a powerful and morally superior America and a marginalized Eastern Europe, the source of criminals and victims.

Eastern Europe and the Philippines are depicted mainly as places of destruction, poverty, and crime, and the people there either as perpetrators or so distressed that they have lost their ability for sound moral judgment. The camera's inquisitive portrayal of Helena and Nadia's apartments, and the living conditions of the Filipino father who sold his daughter, clearly create an impression of desperation. This is not to say that the conditions of women who are being trafficked are not desperate, but if this is the predominant picture of the region and its people (except Helena's mother and Nadia's father), not to mention that the criminals are all Russians, the film creates divisions and perpetuates stereotypes of Eastern Europe as desperate and dangerous. One can argue that the gaze of the camera fixates on denigrating East European living and moral conditions. Most US/Western films, except *Taken*, do not present American trafficked women or domestic trafficking. Instead, they focus on international (East European) people trafficked to the United States or Western Europe, for such presentation more easily utilizes stereotypes to comfort US viewers and project negativity and danger onto the other.

In addition to being aired periodically on the US small screen since its release in 2005, *Human Trafficking* also had international premiers in nine countries, five of them in Western Europe, plus Japan and Australia. The only East European country in which the film had an official premier was Hungary, although its DVD was widely available in all of Eastern Europe. Although I am unsure as to why it had only Hungarian distribution, it is important to point out that the film is well known in Eastern Europe and is used in some prevention campaigns, as shown in my discussion of the Social Club Open Your Eyes in Chapter 2.

In *The New York Times* television section, Alessandra Stanley praises the miniseries. "Particularly on Lifetime, a network for women that is famous for feel-bad escapist melodrama, a movie about sex slavery could easily sag under the weight of cop-show clichés: the headstrong rookie, oafish Russian mobsters and hardened but gold-hearted prostitutes. *Human Trafficking* manages to avoid predictability with sharp, unsentimental writing and exceptionally good acting" (2005). While the acting is truly professional and powerful, one can argue that the writing and especially the structure of the story, confined by the rules of the genre, are in fact predictable. Stanley further offers a bit more nuanced assessment: "*Human Trafficking* is compelling, but it is very much a movie with a message. [...] The criminals and their clients are uniformly sadistic and brutal, and the women they exploit are all unwilling, unknowing victims." Other critics, such as Tom Shales of *The Washington Post*, are less generous in their reviews of the film:

> According to a new miniseries airing on the Lifetime Television
> cable network, trafficking in human beings, young women and
> even children who are railroaded into lives of sexual slavery, is
> globally epidemic and very, very bad. Unfortunately, it is also
> a convenient peg on which to hang a lurid, let's-play-peekaboo
> movie that is also very, very bad—and regularly punctuated
> with scenes of female victims being stripped of their clothes and
> approached menacingly by fat creepy men unbuckling their belts.
> (Shales 2005)

Acknowledging the despicable nature of trafficking, Shales rightly
expresses his disappointment in the film and exposes its flaws mainly
on the level of the script and the temptation of Duguay and producer
Robert Halmi Sr. to titillate the viewer with exposure of the female
body and to also simplify the characters and thus perpetuate stereotypes.

This weakness, clichéd characters (whether US agents or criminals), marks another film, this time a big screen feature, *Taken*. In it,
a former CIA agent appears all-powerful, determined, and above any
moral ambiguity. During a conversation with his buddies, Bryan Mills
(Liam Neeson) expresses satisfaction that he is no longer actively
involved with the agency and can spend more time with his seven-
teen-year-old daughter, Kim, who lives with her mother and stepfa-
ther. Based on his experience, he dislikes the idea of Kim spending
her spring break in Paris with a cousin, but agrees to let her go. The
viewer soon witnesses Kim's kidnapping from a Paris apartment, but
not before she manages to make a call to her dad who records the voice
of the kidnapper. Using his CIA contacts, Mills quickly determines the
name of the criminal, Marko—not surprisingly an Eastern European,
this time Albanian. Mills's associates from CIA Headquarters tell him
that he has 96 hours to rescue his daughter before the trafficking ring
transfers her to an Arab country and he will never see her again.

The film does not portray vulnerable and gullible East European
girls, as the victim comes from a well-off American family. However, she
is kidnapped abroad—a detail which obscures the existence of trafficking
in the United States. Eastern Europe is unfailingly implicated as the
origin of the brutal villains, who meet their deaths in the conflict with
Mills. The viewer observes a lot of armed combat and is also informed

by Mills's former colleague in Paris that Mills has left seven bodies behind. In the *Chicago Sun-Times*, Roger Ebert wrote about the film:

> If CIA agents in general were as skilled as Bryan Mills in particular, Osama bin Laden would have been an American prisoner since late September 2001. *Taken* shows Mills as a one-man rescue squad, a master of every skill, a laser-eyed, sharpshooting, pursuit-driving, pocket-picking, impersonating, knife-fighting, torturing, karate-fighting killing machine who can cleverly turn over a petrol tank with one pass in his car and strategically ignite it with another. (2009)

While the film somewhat exposes the dangers of trafficking, its main objective is to promote the superpowers of US operatives and entertain with its genre typical action scenes. How credible is the presentation of trafficking when a single CIA agent can combat and destroy a whole criminal gang and save his daughter despite the lack of cooperation he receives from the French police? Ebert captures the duality of the film: "It's always a puzzle to review a movie like this. On the one hand, it's preposterous. But who expects a *Bourne*-type city-wrecking operative to be plausible? On the other hand, it's very well-made" (Ebert 2009). Plausibility and credibility do not align with the crime-thriller genre, but the story of trafficking should.[3] Since *Taken* is an action film, its objective is not to inform audiences or raise awareness about this social and human rights problem. The film, however, is used to such end. Even the United Nations Global Initiative to Fight Trafficking website lists it as a film on human trafficking (UN.GIFT).

A EuropaCorp production directed by Pierre Morel and co-written by Luc Besson, *Taken* grossed $145 million in the United States and $77 million in other countries. This French production, centering on the power of an American agent, might surprise the viewer, who is aware of the film's French origin. In the review of the film in *Moving People, Moving Images*, Brown, Iordanova, and Torchin write: "Albanians and Arabs may lazily be cast here

---

[3] *Taken 2* further exploits the genre to the extent that it communicates much more as an action-crime-thriller than informs about trafficking.

as the villains of the piece, but how much this film is an American or a French fantasy about being able to carry out senseless acts of violence against Eastern Europeans and Middle Easterners is open to debate. In other words, the film is highly xenophobic and racist at times, but is it revealing to us the xenophobia and racism of the makers or their imagined versions of the protagonists and audiences?" (2010, 212). An answer to this question might be only speculation, but from the box-office success it is clear that viewers liked the film and found points of identification with the violence, the power of the former-CIA agent, or the latent xenophobia and racism. Similar to *Human Trafficking*, *Taken* constructs the image of the United States (in the role of Mills) as the undefeated, all-powerful force ready to restore justice at all costs.

Contrary to *Taken*, which is uncritical of the role of the West, unfailingly functioning as the creator of trafficking demand, *Sex Traffic* unabashedly exposes the malevolence of the West and its corrupt institutions.[4] The critique of the Western harmful involvement in the continuously expanding scale of trafficking appears very pronounced in the Canadian-British production of the BBC miniseries. Jason Deans reports that "more than 2 million viewers stuck with *Sex Traffic*, Channel 4's harrowing drama about the sexual exploitation of young Eastern European women in London" (2004). One can safely presume that some of the production aspects (Canadian Broadcasting Corporation, federal and commercial support, in combination with the British Channel 4, a commercially funded but public network) contributed to a more critical and nuanced presentation of trafficking without the usual attributes of an optimistic presentation of trafficking outcomes and a black-and-white construction of characters.

Director David Yates, in a dark and tense television drama, skillfully interweaves several intriguing plotlines: the stories of two Moldovan sisters, Elena and Vara, sold to traffickers by Vara's boyfriend, and of a worker at London-based NGO Speak for Freedom, Daniel Appleton, who tries to save the women but realizes with frustration that his organization still depends on funds from corporations involved

---

[4] For a more detailed review of the film and its production side, see Brown, Iordanova, Torchin (2010), 178–179.

in trafficking. One corporation, the Boston-based Kernwell, though it deploys peacekeepers to the International Police Coalition in Bosnia, is revealed to be behind the criminal ring. Apparently, Yates' abilities to confront dark topics and produce a complex world of conflict and intrigue landed him four installments of *Harry Potter* (*The Order of the Phoenix, Half-Blood Prince,* and *Deathly Hallows* Parts 1 and 2). To the questions as to how the producers of *Harry Potter* picked him and what the director of a tough, edgy television drama has that appealed to the producers of an intricately plotted children's fantasy adventure, he answers: "I think they wanted to do a *Harry Potter* that felt realer, and more grown up" (Pulver 2010).

In *Sex Traffic*, which won the 2005 BAFTA for Best Drama Serial, Yates employs his skills to create a plausible and at the same time multi-layered story with multi-dimensional characters, as he exposes the global corporate economy as the main perpetrator of trafficking. The destinies of several trafficked women are interwoven in the narrative, and while the aim of the film appears to be the exposure of the web of global capital, the director carefully depicts women's situations and individualizes their characters, especially Elena and Vara. The scenes of denigrating and humiliating auctions of women and the psychological threats and physical abuse they suffer at the hands of their pimps convincingly speak of their suffering and their trauma, which affect them differently (Plates 8 and 9). While Elena harbors hopes for returning home, Vara, who has assumed a higher position in the operation and seems to understand that there is no escape from this vicious cycle, refuses to return.

"Indeed, as characters cross paths with circuits overlapping and intersecting, the film visualizes the new sovereigns of this transnational terrain: corporate and private entities that supplant states and humans in practices of contemporary governance" (Brown, Iordanova, Torchin 2010, 173). This accurate observation notwithstanding, it is important to note that the Kernwell Corporation is based in Boston, thus exposing the United States as the leader of global capitalism with its inhumane practices. Kernwell's role as leading the trafficking operation resembles the real involvement of the American DynCorp and Halliburton, the US government and particularly the Pentagon's subcontractors, in sex slavery. In 2005, US Congress Representative Cynthia McKinnley confronted then Defense Secretary Donald Rumsfeld and asked him whether it is the government's policy to award US funds to corporations that buy and sell girls and women.[5]

Unlike *Taken*, for instance, a French production which glorifies the superpower of CIA agents and uncritically promotes violence as the solution to effective combat with trafficking, *Sex Traffic* situates the responsibility within the United States, but also renders bare the global interconnectedness of capital in all parts of the world and in all spheres of social life, as it uncovers the London-based non-profit Speak for Freedom's dependence on the donations of Kernwell. While Brown, Iordanova, Torchin acknowledge that *Sex Traffic* "produces a significantly different portrait of the trafficking economy than another miniseries released at around the same time," they also conclude that the film "demonstrates cynicism and ambivalence" (2010, 176–178). Exploring the production aspects of the film and especially the fusion of private and public partnerships (the case of the British Channel 4 or the Canadian Broadcast Corporation employing private networks' marketing strategies), they write: "Appropriately, then, the series is rife with the expression of restraints, providing an illusion of a global economy that is violently and frustratingly privatized, diminishing the autonomy of both publics and public options" (2010, 179) (Plate 10). In addition to the production context and public and private interaction, one can speculate that the film's critical view of global capitalism, led by the United States, reveals some of the anti-American sentiments that have emerged in Europe in the last decade. Perhaps it also exposes an old European perception of America (and Russia for that matter) as "culturally inferior latecomers to the table of world power," and the US "as a crass, business-oriented new world power" (Chatterjee and Holmgren, 2013, 3). Despite this, *Sex Traffic* remains one of the most complex representations of trafficking as it tries to avoid simplicities and stereotypes.

Also critical of the Western involvement as a driving force of trafficking is *The Whistleblower*. The film opens with the main character, Kathryn Bolkovac, a dedicated Nebraska police officer who is disappointed by the fact that her daughter is moving away with her father,

---

[5] "Cynthia McKinney Grills Donald Rumsfeld" (Pumpitout 2011). Rebroadcast of C-SPAN coverage: https://www.youtube.com/watch?v=yMG65jYlDU8 [last accessed: September 15, 2016].

her legal guardian. Bolkovac fails to get a transfer in the police force and move closer to her daughter. Frustrated, she signs a one-year contract to serve as a UN peacekeeper in postwar Bosnia with hopes that the salary will allow her to relocate. In Bosnia, instead of rebuilding a devastated country, she uncovers trafficked women and crimes perpetrated by peacekeeping forces, a dangerous reality of corruption and manipulations, and the undetectable network of private contractors and multinational diplomatic maneuvering. Directed by first-time filmmaker Larysa Kondracki, a Canadian with Ukrainian heritage based in New York, the film stars Academy Award winners Rachel Weisz and Vanessa Redgrave, Monica Bellucci, and Academy Award nominee David Strathairn. The film earned Kondracki the audience award for Best Director at the Seattle International Film Festival in 2011.

Produced by Christina Piovesan, Amy Kaufman, and Mandalay Vision's Celine Rattray, the film was distributed by Samuel Goldwyn Films with all US rights. International sales cover all five continents and many countries (Kit 2010). Based on a true story and developed in collaboration with the real-life Bolkovac, the film relentlessly aims to uncover Western institutional corruption and illegal practices. After its release, Kondracki continued her activism in promoting the film and exposing the UN's corrupt structure. Mike Fleming Jr., a reporter for *Deadline/Hollywood*, remarks:

> Samuel Goldwyn Films and director Larysa Kondracki have finally been given a date for a United Nations screening and panel discussion on *The Whistleblower*... Kondracki will take part in the panel discussion along with Madeleine Rees, former UN rights lawyer and secretary of the Women's International League For Peace And Freedom (played in the film by Vanessa Redgrave); Susana Malcorra, Under Secretary General, Department of Field Support; and Anne-Marie Orler, Police Adviser, Department of Peacekeeping Operations. The screening and discussion is being hosted by UN Secretary General Ban Ki-moon. (2011)

The panel discussion is available online, and one can hear the accusatory tone of Madeleine Rees: "All what you saw in the film really happened. I was there and I know" (UN 2011). This activism and the film's critique of the negative impact of the UN's involvement in the region after the war in Bosnia create a complex presentation of the Western responsibility for trafficking, comparable to the critique in *Sex Traffic*. (Un)surprisingly and frustratingly, the real-life Bolkovac was hired by the British company DynCorp, a subsidiary of the US based DynCorp Inc., a subject of Congressional hearing in the US, mentioned above. Thus, both *Sex Traffic* and *The Whistleblower* indirectly render the corrupt practices of US and British corporations. In 2001, Antony Barnett and Solomon Hughes wrote in *The Guardian*:

> A former United Nations police officer is suing a British security firm over claims that it covered up the involvement of her fellow officers in sex crimes and prostitution rackets in the Balkans. Kathryn Bolkovac, an American policewoman, was hired by DynCorp Aerospace in Aldershot for a UN post aimed at cracking down on sexual abuse and forced prostitution in Bosnia. She claims she was 'appalled' to find that many of her fellow officers were involved. She was fired by the British company after amassing evidence that UN police were taking part in the trafficking of young women from eastern Europe as sex slaves.

While one of the main objectives of the film was to uncover the West and its institutions and corporations as driving forces of trafficking, the main impression that the viewer carries at the end of the film is delivered through Bolkovac's character: it takes charisma, principles, and determination to stand up for justice. Risking her life and losing her job, she exposes the immoral peacekeeping officers and breaks the trafficking ring. In a scene in which Raya, one of the trafficked women, is hesitant to speak up and reveal her abusers because she does not believe that Bolkovac can do much working for the UN (whose other members are perpetrators), Bolkovac looks her in the eyes and says with resolve: "I am an American police officer and it doesn't matter who I work for; I wouldn't let anybody get away with this." Again, an encouraging portrait of an ordinary US policewoman who dares to stand against the unscrupulous bureaucracy of an organization like the UN can be perceived as reaffirming the unfailingly positive representation of the United States in this film. However, the viewer ought to distinguish the depiction of Kate Morozov, serving the United States as an immigration agent and inspired and guided by her boss, from Kathryn

Bolkovac, who is portrayed as being at odds with her superiors both in the United States, where she could not secure a transfer, and in Bosnia, and who refuses to yield her convictions to institutional pressure.

While in *Human Trafficking*, Kate leads the narrative and is the main protagonist, she still has to consult with and follow the orders of her male boss. *The Whistleblower* breaks the gender hierarchy. While Bolkovac confronts her male colleagues and the perpetrators of trafficking, the female Secretary of the UN Women's International League for Peace and Freedom protects her. To a different degree, both films advance the perception that mostly women sympathize with and protect sex-trafficked persons. More interestingly, while in most instances in these films, the gaze assumes the position of a dominant West, betraying a structure that fails to understand differences in East European societies and cultures, select scenes in the films reveal that the only bearers of the look (not the gaze) are the main female protagonists. While a man and a woman direct *Human Trafficking* and *The Whistleblower* respectively, both directors create their female leads as human beings more eager to relate to different experiences and particularly to suffering, without objectifying the subjects of this suffering. In episodes depicting Morozov and Bolkovac in the company of the trafficked young women, the viewer relates to the Russian or East European girls through the eyes of the American female officers. In these scenes, the camera attentively uncovers the suffering that has marked their faces. In one particular instance, Bolkovac finds trafficked women in the dark backroom of a local bar. The camera aligns with her, warmly looking into these women's eyes and asking them to join her and leave the place. Her look reveals tenderness and care for the trafficked women in an attempt to gain their trust. Such scenes, although rare, present an important reversal of the regular mode of representation, in which the Western gaze generally constructs Eastern Europe and its people as others, into a form of representation where a look expresses interest, concern, and desire to help.

In a somewhat reversed portrayal of vice and criminality, *Eastern Promises* presents Russia and Russians as a major force in a world of transgressions. The film depicts London as a destination site for trafficking and crime brought to it by Russians. It received international acclaim and positive critical reception, winning several awards, including the Audience Prize for best film at the Toronto International Film Festival and the Best Actor award for Viggo Mortensen at the British Independent Film Awards. Similarly to his earlier film, *A History of Violence*, director David Cronenberg, interested in the dark side of human nature, focuses on a Russian mafia family's violent inclinations and behavior.

The Russian-born Nikolai Luzhin (Mortensen) is a driver for one of London's Russian organized crime families. Headed by Semion (Armin Mueller-Stahl), the family, including Nikolai, has a history of the Russian *vory v zakone*, a criminal brotherhood forming bonds and abiding by their own rules in prison. Semion owns a Trans-Siberian restaurant, which masks the real nature of the family business: crime and trafficking. The family crosses paths with a midwife at a North London hospital, Anna Khitrova (Naomi Watts), who is deeply affected by the death of a young woman who passes away during childbirth. The woman's Russian language diary leads Anna to Semion's family. After moral dilemmas and ambiguity, brutal violence, and cruelty, it is revealed that Nikolai is a Russian Foreign Service Bureau agent, working with the British Government and a senior police officer. Nikolai has managed to infiltrate the family; he saves Anna, the baby, and becomes the head of the criminal organization. In her review of the film, Doris Toumarkine calls it "essentially a character-driven crime thriller but also a bloody tour de force laced with considerable nudity and sexually bold content" (2007). Although betraying some of the Western perceptions of Eastern Europe as a dangerous region of criminals and victimized women (exemplified in a much more pronounced way in the other films discussed), *Eastern Promises* complicates matters, and the black-and-white presentation of a divided world, with Nikolai's double role but, more importantly, with Cronenberg's talent to subvert genre expectations and delve into the gray area between good and evil, right and wrong.[6] The film suggests the complexities of representing trafficking cases and the difficulties of avoiding

---

[6] Other films, which to a lesser or greater extent reveal a tendency to create a dichotomy of the world, could be discussed here (*Import/Export*, *Transsiberian* [Brad Anderson, US 2008] *Lorna's Silence* [Jean-Pierre Dardenne and Luc Dardenne, Belgium 2008], among others), but because they do not engage with the problem of sex trafficking as their main focus and because reviews in relation to their trafficking content have appeared elsewhere (see Brown, Iordanova, Torchin), I will not elaborate on them.

stereotypes resulting from various global factors and geopolitics, which have created and continue to construct hierarchies, superpowers, and underdogs.

Eastern Europe: Exoticized, Marginalized, and Dangerous

In his book *Inventing Eastern Europe*, Larry Wolff effectively pinpoints the cultural prejudice that drives contemporary, uncomplimentary Western European attitudes towards Eastern Europe in general and towards Russia in particular: "Alienation is in part a matter of economic disparity, the wealth of Western Europe facing the poverty of Eastern Europe, but such disparity is inevitably clothed in the complex windings of cultural prejudice" (1994, 3). In the introduction to the volume *Americans Experience Russia: Encountering the Enigma, 1917 to the Present*, editors Choi Chatterjee and Beth Holmgren "argue that Americans first learn how to write Russia from West European guides, who in turn had learned how to write Russia through their experience in writing Asia and Latin America" (2013, 2). Critically engaging with postcolonial theories, the essays examine America's long experience with Russia—an experience that has existed in a tense parity of temporary allies or political enemies. Focusing on American cultural production and its views of Russia, Chatterjee and Holmgren write: "Popular fiction, film, and, eventually, other mass media variously packaged a cliché-ridden, yet dramatically riveting Russia for American readers and viewers" (2013, 6). All the complexities of the anti-trafficking films and the social investment of their creators notwithstanding, the representation of Eastern Europe and Russia in these films echoes "a cliché-ridden, yet dramatically riveting" construction, which (un)surprisingly has inherited the long tradition of perceptions and representations of self and other.

As discussed above, *The Whistleblower* does not spare its attack on UN peacekeepers in Bosnia and the corrupt and inefficient structure of the UN, but it also offers a few scenes that negatively portray social conditions and relationships in Bosnia. As the director explains: "Locations are a character. Especially in a story such as this, where it's more about what you don't see, so you need to create that world. A lot of it is Kathy putting these clues together... That sense of discovery, that process of Kathy putting together all these worlds and how they connect, it's something you can only really get on location" (Covering Media 2011). Obviously, attention to locations and authenticity are crucial for the credibility of the story. The destruction from the war has left a visible mark both on the urban landscape, with its dilapidated buildings, and the modest furnishings of Bolkovac's accommodation.

At the same time, however, the viewer observes scenes revealing the complicity of local citizens and their appalling and destructive participation in trafficking. Whether this behavior also results from the experience of war, which desensitizes people, is left to the viewer. The film shows the collapse of the values and moral judgment of local men. Local police receive bribes from bar owners to remain silent and provide protection for the traffickers to maintain their "business" undisturbed. While the film presents a Bosnian policeman who is trying to assist Bolkovac, other policemen are indifferent or complicit (Plates 11 and 12). Although these scenes are not numerous, they still suggest that Eastern Europe—from Ukraine, where the main protagonists were trafficked, to Bosnia—is a community of victims and criminals. That being said, I ought to stress that the film mostly aims to portray Western entanglement, uncovering not only the corruption of the UN and its subcontractors, but also the dishonesty and involvement of ordinary officers, who threaten and intimidate Bolkovac for her attempts to protect the trafficked women. The film appears critical of both sides of the divide, West and East, thus elevating even more the decency, sense of fairness, and fighting spirit of Bolkovac, an ordinary American police woman.

Unlike *The Whistleblower*, *Human Trafficking* clearly stereotypes Eastern Europe as the other, while remaining uncritical of the West's negative involvement in trafficking and positioning the United States as the main force to combat and defeat this crime. Four minutes into the film, the camera jump-cuts and the viewer is offered a panoramic establishing shot of Charles Bridge in Prague with titles, confirming the location. With a four-second pan, the camera directs its gaze to a busy street with streetcars and crowded sidewalks to zoom in and focus on a medium shot of a homeless beggar. From there the camera continues to move from left to right, slowly revealing what appears to be a basement room converted into living quarters. The viewer remembers the beggar on the sidewalk, and behind the ground-level small window the spectator is introduced to one of the main female characters, Helena (smoking), and her five-year old daughter. From a door window, the rest of the underground quarters, which obviously function as a workshop, are visible (Plate 13).

The film introduces the next trafficking victim, Nadia from Ukraine, in a similar manner. After the scene with Helena, the camera jumps to Ukraine, revealing truly dilapidated street conditions with Soviet era cars. After Nadia participates in a modeling agency's recruitment session, she runs home with trepidation as to how she could tell her father. Although much bigger than Helena's basement room, Nadia and her father's apartment (Plate 14) is large but old and with obvious marks of poverty; one larger room functions as kitchen, dining, and living space, separated by a French door from the only other room in the house. These depressing conditions are reinforced by the father's admission that "these last years have been tough."

Although with alterations, these presentations resemble Western films about the travels of Westerners to unknown Asian or African countries. The Western travellers, agents of a superior gaze (representing culture and civilization), usually meet nature and barbarism in these encounters. In Paul Glaser's *The Air Up There* (1994), the main protagonist, Jimmy Dolan, travels to Africa in search of a basketball player with a flawless physique. In one scene, he is so thrilled by the landscape and the wild animals that he pulls out a camera and begins filming. The shot resembles a carefully designed postcard (Kaplan 1997, 75–77). From the magnificent view of Charles Bridge, a Gothic stone bridge that connects the Old Town and Lesser Town (Malá Strana), a landscape that signifies the rich past of the city, the camera zooms in on the underground living quarters. With one pan the director acknowledges the glorious Czech history, in a panoramic shot that looks like a postcard, but quickly focuses on the terrible present. The camera does not attempt to relate to these conditions and tell the story behind them, but it quickly gazes at them, satisfied with the exposure of poverty and misery. Since the camera tends to objectify and gaze at East European people and conditions, the film is not interested in establishing a connection between economic decline and people's desperation, which appears more as naïveté. There is no doubt that the intention was to reveal the hardship of women who become prey to traffickers, but one can argue that the lingering camera gazes at these conditions rather than looks at them, perpetuating stereotypes about "underdeveloped" Eastern Europe. This first impression can be contrasted by the way Kate relates to the Eastern European women with understanding and compassion, a relation that adds ambiguity to the depiction of Eastern Europe and its people. One can speculate that this ambiguity reveals the creators and producers' conflicting attitudes: on the one hand, they present Eastern Europe as a place of economic and social decline where naïveté guides people's decisions; on the other, they individualize to a certain degree the trafficked women in their relation to Kate in select scenes in which the camera aligns with her caring look.

The construction of Russia in Lilya 4-ever appears more disturbing. Although considered one of the most effective anti-trafficking feature films and often used in anti-trafficking awareness campaigns, more than other Western productions Lilya 4-ever objectifies and exoticizes Eastern Europe and in particular Russia. Several scholars have criticized the film for its objectifying gaze.[7] Lars Lyngsgaard Fjord Kristensen in particular calls attention to the West–East division in the film and its construction of post-Soviet Russian young women as "Other and as victim" (2007, 5). The film presents the devastating economic conditions in Russia. At the same time, the particular reasons for Lilya's vulnerability appear to be a series of betrayals by her mother, aunt, friend, teacher, and social worker—all female characters. Her sole attempt to break away from this deception is to frequent a local bar and to try (not very successfully) to pick up clients. Soon, even this agency is taken away from her when she falls in love with a "loverboy"/pimp, who traffics her to Sweden. Suchland convincingly argues:

> The failure of the postsocialist state is that it could not provide for the mother and now cannot help keep its daughter from being raped. The audience does not view Sweden as the sole perpetrator of Lilya's victimization. By the time she arrives in Sweden, the girl has experienced grueling emotional and physical trauma. (2013, 373)

---

[7] For detailed and perceptive analyses of the film, see Kristensen (2007), Suchland (2013), and Schuckman-Matthews (2015).

While I agree with Suchland that the film mostly places the blame on the failure of the Russian state and society, I ought to stress that the demand side is also exposed in the images of the Swedish clients. In addition to Suchland's critique directed at the portrayal of the deteriorated Russian state, I contend that the collapse of the moral foundation of Russian society appears even more problematic (although they are interrelated). A considerable part of the film's narrative depicts a series of dishonest and wicked betrayals and cruel disregard for humanity and civility, all of which create the conditions for Lilya's situation. In these depictions, the gaze takes over from the look, for there is no desire to understand and relate to Lilya's environment and situation. While the state is also implicated, as Suchland posits, the main concern lies with the mother's decision to abandon her daughter—a very personal and brutal choice—which might be motivated by economic hardship, but the film does not reveal it as such. It only depicts a mother who opts for a life in the United States with her new husband and whose words—that they cannot take Lilya but will invite her later—ring false.

The scene of the mother's departure for the United States depicts Lilya kneeling in mud and being approached by a street dog, which obviously fills the emotional space left by her departing mother (Plate 15, 16, 17, and 18). It is hard to find a stronger indictment against a community than the one presented in this scene. And this is only the beginning of Lilya's experience with human malice and cruelty. Although the film critiques the male Swedish consumers of sexual services, portrayed with disgust through Lilya's eyes, as the gaze of the camera in these scenes aligns with her, the projection of blame to the Russian state is stronger. Lilya's trafficking abuse and rapes are devastating, but the emotional trauma had already been inflicted in Russia.

My discussion of these few selected films indicates that although driven by different production demands, market expectations, and genre constraints, they all tell the story of trafficking while (un)willingly (re)creating stereotypes of the West and of Eastern Europe. Some directors strive to achieve a truthful presentation of the scale of this human rights violation and to raise awareness, but often their good intentions yield to traditional constructs of the world or ideological agendas. Although most films include narrative titles at the beginning or the end, with truthful data about the scale of trafficking (usually quantitative), this measure cannot always restore the objectivity of the portrayal. *The Whistleblower* ends with a scene of Bolkovac's interview with the BBC, no doubt attempting to alter the genre and add a documentary feel to it. Her interview is interspersed with images of the trafficked women (which appear as though in Kathy's mind). This scene shows that a court found her dismissal unfair, and to the question, "Would you do it again?" she replies with voice-over, while the viewer watches the two young victims dancing and laughing in slow motion, "Yes, I will. No doubt!" This scene is followed by narrative titles stating that a number of implicated peacekeepers were sent home but none faced criminal charges, a sign of the film's striving for realism. *Human Trafficking*, too, ends with a factual reminder about the victims of trafficking, but its depiction of trafficking reveals mostly stereotypes, thus rendering the film ineffective. Its ending cannot change the overall impression about the conditions and forces of trafficking that it creates, and the brief inclusion of "reality" cannot repair the stereotypes that the crime drama offers. While Carrie Baker reaches similar conclusions in her article "Moving Beyond 'Slaves, Sinners, and Saviors': An Intersectional Feminist Analysis of US Sex-Trafficking Discourses, Law and Policy," my analysis explores the mechanisms of such constructions and driving forces different from the ones identified by Baker:

> When placed side by side, the portrayals of sex trafficking by the US government, anti-trafficking organizations, and the media exhibit some common patterns, but also distinctions. All three tend to focus on sexually vulnerable and helpless women and girls in need of protection and rescue. Whereas the government discourses frame the state or professionals as rescuers, anti-trafficking organizations and the media focus on individual male rescuers. Hollywood distinguishes itself with an extreme and hypermasculinized version of the trafficking rescue narrative, where the rescuer is a former law enforcement officer turned vigilante and playing outside the rules. In all three mediums, race and nationality play out in predictable ways, with white Western men rescuing women and girls, often in developing countries, from traffickers who are men of color or Eastern Europeans. These stories reiterate conservative beliefs and values around gender, sexuality, and nationality. (2013, 17)

While I identify some of the problems Baker outlines above in my discussion of the films, I also point out to different depictions and framing of the trafficking scenario. Not only do male characters appear as rescuers and women, although again American, lead the fight against trafficking, they show true sensitivity to the trafficked people and do not objectify their suffering or bodies. In addition, not all Western productions position the state or professionals as rescuers, as some critically depict their entanglement with trafficking.

Media Documentaries

Paying attention to the selection of material (trafficking cases) and data presented, this section examines media reports and documentaries broadcast on television. Documentaries subject to my analysis include Frontline's *Sex Slaves*, CNN's *Not My Life*, Al Jazeera's *Slavery: A 21st Century Evil*, and the Rescue and Restore program *Look Beneath the Surface: Identifying Victims of Human Trafficking in the U.S.* The selection of these four documentaries was motivated by my interest in discussing media which present different (from one other) approaches to the story of trafficking and which were produced by some of the most respected media venues such as the Public Broadcasting Service (PBS), Frontline, and CNN. Frontline was established in 1983 and hailed upon its debut on PBS as "the last best hope for broadcast documentaries," while *Newsday* praised it as "television's last fully serious bastion of journalism," according to Frontline's website. Whereas Frontline's *Sex Slaves* documentary represents "serious" journalism, CNN is widely considered the most watched global news broadcast and, thus, the most popular. By analyzing *Sex Slaves* and *Not My Life*, I cover some of the most ambitious broadcast documentary projects available to wide audiences. Finding a niche for offering an alternative view to the dominant Western outlook on the world, Al Jazeera has gained popularity and respect not only in the Middle East and Africa, but in the West as well. Its documentary affords an angle on the trafficking story ignored or avoided by Western productions. Last, Rescue and Restore is a program funded by the US Department of Health and Human Services working to educate and train hundreds of local community, faith-based, or social services organizations. *Look Beneath the*

Surface is a short, fifteen-minute documentary designed to raise awareness and train local activists, social workers, and police force how to
recognize trafficking victims and assist them.

Produced in 2007, *Sex Slaves* appeared as one of the first thoroughly researched and detailed documentaries presenting trafficking
not only as a horrific crime and experience, but also revealing many of
its complexities and the difficulties that prevent effective combat.[8] The
documentary opens with a close-up of fingers counting money and
a voice-over announcing:

> These women have been torn from their families. They have been
> sold into slavery. They are victims of a multi-billion-dollar inter-
> national business that traffics hundreds of thousands of women
> a year. Tonight Frontline takes a hidden camera deep inside the
> global sex trade. Frontline also follows one man who is deter-
> mined to get his wife back before she is lost for good to the world
> of the traffickers. It's an extraordinary journey that raises tough
> questions about governments around the world largely indifferent
> to the traffickers' abuses.

These introductory lines are accompanied by images of young women
in nightclubs or police raids rescuing women from hidden basement
rooms. After this introduction, which presents the main aspects of trafficking to be followed in the film, the camera focuses on the face of
a young woman saying through tears: "Before this I hadn't encoun-
tered much evil in the world." A few minutes into the film, the viewer
has already learned that trafficking is slavery and a multi-billion dollar
global business, and that survivors will tell its story. Intriguingly, the
filmmakers also hint at the adventure story that they have built into the
narrative, mentioning a hidden camera and also the fact that the story
will follow a man in search of his trafficked wife. Unsurprisingly, this
temptation to build tension reminds the reader about the previously
discussed feature films which all, to a greater or lesser extent, succumb
to the same desire to produce a thriller (or crime-action) and, thus,

---

[8] The shorter, 1997 documentary *Bought and Sold* likewise offers a more
nuanced perspective, encouraging the West to address its complicity in sex
trafficking. Similarly, see Mimi Chakarova's *The Price of Sex* (2011).

jeopardize some aspects of the trafficking story. Documentaries, too, often tend to cater to audiences' expectations—a sign of the effect of market pressure and ideology.

The stories of trafficking survivors begin in Odessa, Ukraine. The city's seaport has been used regularly to traffic women into Turkey, where a visa is not required for Ukrainian or Moldovan citizens (the viewer is informed). The film unfolds as personal stories of survivors are intertwined with the realities depicted by the hidden camera that follows a Ukrainian woman, Olga, who lures other women with promises for jobs in Turkey and then sells them there. The film also tells the story of Tania, who comes from an impoverished family with terminally sick siblings, and after being rescued and staying at home for a while, she decides to return to Turkey, for this is her only option to help her brother and sister. Very few films attempt to inform the viewer that some of the trafficked women return to prostitution on their own accord or become pimps after escaping. These difficult situations have economic and psychological explanations but filmmakers tend to stay away from them, for they demand a more in-depth study and engagement with social and economic realities as well as family, individual, and psychological factors for the existence of trafficking.[9] At the same time, her return to prostitution does not mean that she is trafficked. Here, the Western moral judgment again betrays its double standards. As Jacqueline Berman puts it: "[I]t risks positioning US and European sex workers as capable of 'choosing' this work in the towns and cities of the industrialized west, while women from developing countries in these same industries and locations are seen as forced, exploited, tricked, and trafficked" (2004, 47).[10]

From *Sex Slaves* the viewer learns about the mechanisms of deception and recruitment of future victims and their horrific experiences. Interviews with the producer, and a pimp who agrees to participate after he was sentenced to a five-year probation, provide additional

---

[9] See, for example, the work of Zimmerman et al. (2007 and 2008), which has shown why some victims are psychologically inclined to repeat the violent situation. Some of the young women come from families with persistent history of violence.

[10] For other misplaced and inadequate perceptions of trafficking, see Davies (2009).

information about the ways pimps "break" the young women with violence and psychological blackmail, saying that they will harm their loved ones at home. The sentenced pimp mentions that 70 percent of the young women who go abroad seeking job opportunities through unreliable and suspicious venues know very well what they will be doing there, that is, prostituting. The problem with this "revelation" is not that there are no such cases, but that the documentary presents trafficked women as either naïve or with questionable morality. The violation of human rights in trafficking lies in the nature of the abuse, depriving women of their freedom and keeping them in servitude forcefully. Whether some women suspect that they might be asked to prostitute abroad is beside the point. What drives or characterizes trafficking, not prostitution, is coercion, psychological abuse, or physical violence.[11]

In addition, *Sex Slaves* contains some outdated or misleading information for the viewer of the mid-2010s. The producer states that the disappearance of the Soviet system of socialism and the new liberal border regimes are the main reason for the trafficking of women from the former Soviet Union. While these factors aided trafficking to a certain degree, the true reasons are different—namely, the division of the world into developed and well-off countries that drive demand, and economically underdeveloped regions (all newly independent states emerging after the collapse of the Soviet Union), which provide the supply. For example, in 2005 Gail Kligman and Stephanie Limoncelli explained: "As in other forms of labor migration, poverty, and limited economic opportunities are primary factors in the lives of women and girls who are trafficked, voluntarily or not" (128). These details— framing the trafficking story within the political collapse of the Eastern Bloc and the Soviet Union, as well as the adventure subplot—do not add any significant information and mostly create narrative tension, and the questionable views on East European women are misleading.

Six years later, after trafficking gained more attention, CNN International ran promotional clips dedicated to its Freedom Project. In 2012, CNN undertook a large project, launching a website with

---

[11] A complete definition of trafficking can be found in the Introduction of this book.

various journalistic reports, short clips, data, articles, and documentaries dedicated to the problems of trafficking. No other media corporation has ever engaged so closely and thoroughly with trafficking as
CNN, and this, no doubt, deserves credit. One of their promotional
clips begins with a scene of heavily armed police breaking into a shady
building, while a voice-over commands: "In action and get answers."
The promo ends with a young man sitting at his laptop, typing and
looking at the screen. The voice-over, this time much more direct,
narrates: "A CNN story outraged him, compelled him to take action,
to take down a corporation." And after a pause, titles appear: "The
CNN Freedom Project. Be inspired. 2012." Undoubtedly, the clip is
designed to promote the power of journalism, and more specifically,
CNN, to affect and inspire people to take part in the fight against trafficking. It also transmits encouragement and hope: one can take down
a corporation; we can end this modern-day slavery. Another clip presents a montage of brief reporting lines of investigative journalists, each
speaking about his or her particular case of trafficking. These succinct
stories are connected by an animation of a child's paper plane flying
across the screen with the following titles: "Modern Day Slavery,"
"CNN is taking a stand," "To make a difference," "Join us as we go
beyond borders to end modern day slavery," "We've questioned,"
"Challenged," "All over the world." CNN's other numerous promos
aim to achieve the same encouraging and uplifting effect—despite the
horrors of this modern-day slavery and its growing proportions, there is
hope as long as we all take a stand.

Similarly hopeful and encouraging is the message of the CNN
documentary *Not My Life*. Compared to *Sex Slaves*, *Not My Life* moves
beyond the topic of trafficking for sexual exploitation—a constructive
step, since most media attention has been paid to sex trafficking for
reasons mentioned in the introduction, such as the dual goal of most
media products to raise awareness as well as reach larger audiences
(and in most cases seek to make profit). In this respect, focusing on
trafficking as a form of slavery for domestic servitude or labor exploitation of minors, the film reveals lesser-known aspects of trafficking.
While *Sex Slaves* focused on young women from Ukraine and Moldova
being sold in Turkey and left the United States out of the picture of
trafficking altogether, *Not My Life* rightly includes two stories of
women trafficked in the United States (one domestically and the other

internationally), bringing to light an important fact largely ignored until recently—namely that the United States is not an exception to trafficking.

The documentary opens with voice-over on a black screen: several experts or activists briefly explain what trafficking is about and the misconceptions around it. The first story interwoven in the film presents the life of Lake Volta (Ghana) teenage boys, who have been bought and exploited in fisheries and who either lose their lives entangled in fishing nets or remain for years enslaved to the local industry's lord. Narrating the stories, Glenn Close begins with the following statement: "Of all the cruel and evil things human beings do to one another in the world today, nothing is more inhuman that the trafficking and enslavement of our planet's youth." Although powerful and effectively narrated, no doubt, this statement frames the problem within the moral frame of good and evil. Close to the end of the film, Grace, one of the survivors originally abducted as a twelve-year-old girl and forced to be a soldier, with tears in her eyes says that she could not understand how grown-ups could be using children in armed conflicts, raping children, and destroying the future. She struggles to comprehend how such evil exists. Close provides the filmmakers' response: "The simplest answer to Grace's question is that there's always been a struggle between good and evil in the world and always will be, but in this struggle there is hope."

Combining interviews of experts and survivors with footage from various places in the world, mostly connected to the stories of the survivors, the filmmakers encouragingly show young resilient people who have managed to escape their servitude and overcome their traumas. Kevin Bales, President of the organization Free the Slaves and author of several books on trafficking, is shown saying how marvelously resilient these young people are. After Close's summation, socially engaged individuals (sister Eugenia from the Italian Union of Major Superiors and Leo Sakamoto, a Human Rights Advocate from Brazil) plead with viewers that we all are responsible and have to take action. The end of the film presents silent images of the survivors, while their current situations as functioning individuals are conveyed via narrative titles. All this paired with Close's last word about hope unambiguously transmits the message that if we all become engaged, trafficking can be eradicated and there is hope. Underlying CNN's overall approach, this view of trafficking intends to be inspirational, but one can certainly argue how helpful it is to focus on the moral causes rather than on the economic and political ones, and suggest hope when there is very little hope for the decline of trafficking as well as for the trafficked people. Choosing to frame trafficking as a story of survival can even be called irresponsible, since the ratio of survivors to victims who never recover overwhelmingly shows that recovery is an exception rather than the norm (Plate 19).[12]

Al Jazeera adopts a very different approach that shapes the message of *Slavery: A 21ˢᵗ Century Evil.* It is a project with a dedicated website and a documentary consisting of seven episodes.[13] Although the moral concept of "evil" exists in the title, the film rather rationally and with concepts of supply, demand, and profit frames the existence of trafficking. I will comment on one episode that focuses on sex trafficking.

The filmmakers' intentions and ideology become obvious from the very opening of the episode. Animation changes a black-and-white drawing of what appears to be centuries-old ships into colored images of real ships, perhaps museum exhibits. The camera focuses on the leading journalist Rageh Omaar on the deck of one of the ships, telling the viewers that "for three hundred years the most powerful nations on earth grew even richer and stronger on the profit of the slave trade," and "twelve million men, women, and children were forcibly transported from Africa on slave ships like this to the colonies and plantations of North and South America" (Plate 20). From the very beginning, both visually and verbally, the film frames trafficking as a modern form of slavery and implicates the powerful nations in the world that profit from it. To reinforce the connection between trafficking and slavery, the next scene shows close-ups of iron chains, while Omaar states that today slavery as trafficking is alive and thriving. This introduction is followed by a brief emotional testimony of a survivor from Moldova. The technique, familiar to the viewer, of intertwining survivors' testimonies with interviews of experts is utilized in this film, too, but with a very different goal—to expose the responsibility of developed

---

[12] See Zimmerman et al. (2007 and 2008).

[13] For more about the project, see http://www.aljazeera.com/programmes/slaverya21stcenturyevil/ [last accessed: July 25, 2016].

Western countries for the existence and proliferation of trafficking in the twenty-first century. Bales is again one of the experts featured in this film, but unlike his optimistic statements in *Not My Life*, emphasizing the strength and resilience of survivors, here he only provides data, namely, "Around the world our best estimate is that 27 million people are being trafficked and from them about 6-8 percent is sex trafficking." With this statistic in the background, the story of trafficking is presented as a story of two countries: the Netherlands, developed and liberal, where many sex trafficked women end up, and the other, Moldova, poor and underdeveloped, from where many young women are being coerced or forcibly trafficked. The story of a young Moldovan woman, Dorina, begins and ends with poverty. Dorina narrates her traumatic experience during the first five minutes of the documentary, and a voice-over states that she is a lucky survivor who receives social assistance and help from the La Strada office in Moldova. From there, the film uncovers the mechanisms of recruitment with false job ads in local newspapers with commentary by La Strada staff members. The undercover journalists connect with local pimps (one of them Kavali) and expose their tactics. Next, the focus shifts to a Turkish trafficker, Baran, and his organized ring which trafficked hundreds of Eastern European women to Amsterdam. *Slavery: A 21ˢᵗ Century Evil* blends trafficking and sex work and blames the liberal positions of the Netherlands in perpetuating this "evil." The last interview in the film is with John R. Miller, US Anti-Trafficking Ambassador from 2003 to 2006, who argues that Holland is the cause, not the solution to trafficking and the legalization of prostitution only adds to the abuse of women. In a direct accusation, Miller states that the Dutch took the same approach in the seventeenth century, boasting they "had the healthiest slave ships" (that is, providing the best conditions for their slaves), but this was only an excuse to avoid abolition. The film takes its critique a step further by accusing the US government of favorably rating the Netherlands for their measures to prevent trafficking because of its status as a developed Western country, but ranks Moldova lower, which in turn might trigger economic sanctions against it. The last voice-over powerfully passes judgment: "Until the rich Western countries address the demand for prostitution rather than profit from it there will always be men like Kavali and Baran, and there always will be sex slaves…" Although commendable for its vehement exposure of the West's involvement in trafficking, the clear ideological stand of *Slavery: A 21ˢᵗ Century Evil* blurs the difference between sex work and trafficking and deprives women of their free will and agency. Thus, this documentary is yet another example of ideologically driven presentations of trafficking that jeopardize the fight against trafficking rather than help in creating well-informed and socially engaged viewers.

Last, this discussion explores some aspects of the US government's and more particularly the Department of Health and Human Services, anti-trafficking campaign through the organization Rescue and Restore and its video *Look Beneath the Surface*. The goal of the organization and the video is to raise awareness about trafficking and to educate communities, law enforcement personnel, and social workers to recognize trafficking situations and assist trafficked persons. The video opens with narrative titles stating the enormous scale of trafficking, which exists all over the world and in the United States. A cut introduces the viewers to a survivor, whose hands are only shown but her voice narrates the horrors of her experience. The video (as previous ones discussed) interlinks the testimonies of survivors with statements of experts, like the detective from the New York Police Department Organized Crime Investigation Division, Kevin Mannion, who confirms that trafficked people are not criminals but victims and should be treated as such. Another US government official informs the viewer that these people are eligible for services needed to restore their lives. By detailing ways to recognize trafficked persons and providing specific information (like the National Human Trafficking Resource Center telephone number and other services and organizations), the video aims to function as a guide (or tool kit) for the identification and rescue or trafficked people. The end gives more details about the Rescue and Restore's website and the featured survivors and their current situations as the camera pauses on an American flag. While no doubt informative, this video contains some of the common flaws of media products. For example, it mentions that US citizens can also be trafficked but tells the stories of children from Latin America and Africa only. I recognize that its objective is to educate communities and professionals on how to identify and rescue trafficked people, but the information it provides is too general and therefore even misleading. While social assistance (legal and medical) exists for rescued trafficked persons, they have no access to psychological help and counseling, which they need as much as everything else. Similarly to the CNN products, this video frames the trafficking experience as a story of survivors and engaged US communities that can make a difference.

This chapter analyzed the production, profit, and ideology in the feature films' portrayal of trafficking. My discussion of several films—all Western productions—reveals that the depiction of trafficking is subject to various levels of construction of human trafficking as a story unfolding within the dichotomy of East versus West. This portrayal sometimes critiques the Western contribution to the proliferation of trafficking, but more often objectifies Eastern Europe as land of social and moral demise, and elevates the West as a moral beacon and its law enforcement agents as rescuers. The camera in these films more often than not gazes at Eastern Europe, exposing disinterest in knowing its differences and anxieties about the perceived threats coming from it. A few select scenes in *The Whistleblower* (and to a lesser degree in *Human Trafficking*) offer the only exception, as through the female leads the camera engages in relations with trafficked East European persons.

The documentaries and media products betray ideological agendas that frame the trafficking stories, too. Subjectivity and opinions rather than observation, verifiable evidence, and objective reporting shape the documentaries discussed here. Each of these documentaries suffers from a main structural problem: they rely on the testimonials of survivors interlaced with the statements of experts. This structure places the survivors on display, even if their faces are blurred, while the experts, usually male, analyze or interpret their situations. As Myra Macdonald observed about women's voices in British documentaries, personal experience can merely function as "an illustration of the argument developed from other sources" (2009, 670). Guided by ideology and profit, these documentary-makers turn personal experience into commodification and choose to focus on some aspects of trafficking and to ignore others.

CHAPTER 5

East European Feature Films and NGO Media

In the previous chapter I concluded that, despite their good intentions and different levels of success, most Western film productions about trafficking gaze at East European societies and their peoples, constructing them as others. Most unproductive is the fixation on the region as a source of criminals and victims. This portrayal of trafficking negatively impacts awareness campaigns and their attempts to create informed viewers who can take action against trafficking. Even worse, they drive ineffective policies that focus on fighting organized crime and strengthening security, policies that disregard human rights issues and approach trafficked persons only as naïve victims.

At the same time, I mentioned earlier that the process of othering is not a trademark of the West. Neumann studied Russian collective identity formation in relation to Europe from the Napoleonic wars and the Decembrist uprising (1825) to the 1990s, and found evidence of the Russian debate about its relation to Europe as early as the midfifteenth century (Neumann 1996). The Cold War years intensified the debate, and the arts, guided by the doctrine of socialist realism, denounced the West and portrayed it mostly as a dangerous enemy. As mentioned in the introduction, excellent examples of scholarship investigating the Russian cinematic construction of the United States as villain are Youngblood and Shaw's *The Cinematic Cold War* and Goscilos' *Fade from Red*.

During the transition to democracy and the Yelstin administration, the economy crumbled and privatization was so mishandled and corrupted as to produce the term *grabification* (from the verb "to grab," signaling the high scale corruption and thievery that defined the process). At that time, the adoption of Western economic models and cultural values, although desired earlier, received negative responses from the impoverished Russian population. A Russian-produced film, Rudolf Fruntov's *All the Things We Dreamed of for so Long* (1997) illustrates this well. The film reveals anti-Western sentiments, evident in the depiction of Western Europe as an evil force endangering and corrupting Russia's youth, sentiments that are also observed today. The attack directed at the West today is exemplified most visibly through the anti-gay propaganda laws introduced by the Putin administration, aiming to penalize everybody who demonstrates same sex affection or love in public. This law, which received some support from the general public, was steeped in the discourse of protecting Russian traditional values against decadent Western influences.

Fruntov's *All the Things We Dreamed of for so Long* focuses on the theme of the Western seductive and destructive power of money. Although the film blurs the line between prostitution and trafficking— a sign of not only misperceptions but also, perhaps, of an abolitionist discourse—it is worth briefly discussing it here. *All the Things We Dreamed of for so Long* presents the story of a young man (Nikolai Dobrynin), who after military service is torn between a life devoid of opportunity and his dreams of success, money, and Western cars. Unexpectedly, he meets an old friend who offers him a large amount of money to do a "job." The young man, overconfident in his abilities, jumps at the opportunity to fulfill his dreams. He is given a new car and is asked to drive it from Germany to Russia without stopping along the way. But while still in Germany, he is lured off course by the first striptease bar he sees. After a while he picks out a girl (Anna Terekhova), who by his estimation is one hundred percent German. The "hero" pays for her and enters her room to discover that she is actually Russian. Very disappointed by this, he wants his money back, begins to fight, and is arrested. The drugs discovered in his car make his situation worse. The prostitute, determined to help him, visits him in prison and develops a plan for his escape. After some adventures, they reunite in the free world and he falls in love with her. The viewer learns that she has become a prostitute not of her own choice but is being trafficked, although the film does not really offer any details about her situation as a trafficked person. More importantly, she is religious and leads the young man to the local Orthodox Church. He has a cathartic experience at his first church visit and is baptized. The audience witnesses his transformation: through the prostitute's love, he discovers the path toward happiness and God. In one of the rare media discussions of the film, the Russian journalist Elena Volkova unmistakably unveils the main protagonist's search for religious faith and love as she alludes to Russian youth's similar pursuits (Volkova 1996). One ought to note here that the revival of the role of the Russian church and the Russian Orthodox religion in the 1990s was seen as a natural process following the communist past, when religious practices were repressed.

The film is intriguing with its numerous references to *Crime and Punishment*—references that work on multiple levels. The director seems to promote the very unique Dostoevskian religious philosophy that the path to God, salvation, and peace is found after committing crime and suffering because of it. The storyline offers a modern interpretation of Raskolnikov's crimes and Sonia's spiritual influence over him. At the beginning of the film the influence of Western money is presented as corrupting the souls and bodies of young Russians. The young man offers himself for sale and, with the money he receives, pays for the girl in the bar. Clearly the capital (money) coming from the West turns the Russian spirit and the Russian people into commodities. To this vulgar economy Russians answer with Dostoevsky, with their faith in "Russianness" and in salvation. Marx argues that in the capitalist mode of production, there is a veil of mystery over commodities that hide their true character. In religion, the same thing occurs. Men create gods, and so much mystery surrounds these gods that men become dominated by them (Marx 1886, 32–34). It seems that in this film, the characters attempt to escape or avoid the mysterious and corruptive nature of the commodities relation, but they seek other mysteries—those of God and spirituality, a Dostoevskian solution. In both cases—the world of religion and of commodities—appearance and illusion pose as reality, whereas reality becomes hidden. Similarly to Western film productions that present stereotypical images of Eastern Europe, this film gazes at Germany, and the viewer sees the glitter of a consumer society that hides moral depravity and corruption, similar to the one-sided construction of the West in Cold War Russian films. With its message of a morally superior Russian society, this film rivals Western productions, advancing the same latent agenda but about Western moral dominance. The female lead exemplifies Russian superiority, for even if Western evil can corrupt her body, her pure soul can withstand it, as she finds solace in a Russian Orthodox (not any other) Church in Germany.

Unlike this rather shallow depiction of trafficking, other Eastern and more specifically South Eastern European films explore the causes and effects of trafficking in South Eastern Europe or the Balkans in much more complex ways. I focus here on three films from the region, *Put lubenica* (*The Melon Route*, director Branko Schmidt, 2006), a production of Croatian Radio-Television; *Sestre* (*Sisters*, director Vladimir Paskaljević and Bojana Maljević, 2011), a Serbian independent production of Monte Royal Pictures International; and *S litse nadolu* (*Face Down*, director Kamen Kalev, 2015), a Bulgarian-French co-production of Waterfront Film and Le Pacte. Other East-West co-productions that deserve attention will be analyzed in the last chapter.

For good reasons, film scholars like Iordanova and Anikó Imre detail the difficulties in presenting and examining East European or Balkan national cinemas as one interrelated corpus of films instead of studying them individually. And yet they embraced the opportunities to produce knowledge on cinemas from the regions, cinemas which relate to each other in more ways than one can grasp at first. In her introduction to *The Cinema of the Balkans*, Iordanova writes:

> A closer examination of Balkan cultural output, however, reveals an astonishing thematic and stylistic consistency. Cinema in particular testifies to a specific artistic sensibility, possibly coming from shared history and socio-cultural space. The issues, across borders, are the same: turbulent history and volatile politics; a semi-Orientalist positioning which some see as marginality, and others define as a crossroad or a bridge between East and West, a series of adverse encounters between Christianity and Islam; a legacy of patriarchy and economic and cultural dependency. (2006, 1)

Similarly, with her *Cinema of the Other Europe: The Industry and Artistry of East European Film*, Iordanova aims "to contribute to two fields of study: first, to European film studies and second to studies of East Central European culture" (2003, 1). Concerned that "with the capitalist world in general and the United States in particular in search of replacement Cold War others to take the Soviet Bloc's strategic position, East European cultures are left with no representational space in the evolving post-Cold War configuration of the global order," in 2005 Imre offered an impressively cohesive volume which outlines similar and related paths of content and aesthetic developments of East European national cinemas (2005, xvi).

In the decade after the publication of Imre's volume, the Russian Federation led by Putin has disturbed the global order about which she writes. In the mid-2010s, Russia slowly but firmly emerged as the United States' main adversary and a new political and military power of considerable significance. The Russian alleged interference in the 2016 US presidential elections and reports about the Russian connections of President Trump's associates add more credence to the new role Russia intends to play on the global stage. This shift in world geo-politics undoubtedly marks Russia's film production evident in such films as Fedor Bondarchuk's *Stalingrad* (2013), for example, which unabashedly re-claims Russia's crucial role in the defeat of Nazi Germany in World War II and extends Russia's contribution to people's wellbeing in the present. The Stalingrad story is framed by references to Russians' participation in the recovery mission after the devastating tsunami in Japan in 2011.

Since I am discussing three South Eastern European films, I will re-focus my attention to anti-trafficking films from the region positioned between the West and Russia's new political battle. Having learned from Iordanova and Imre, I cautiously examine the objectives and aesthetic qualities of these three films from the Balkans as they relate to one another and reveal common concerns about their national communities in relation to the problem of trafficking. There is no doubt that these representations are borne out from the region's relatively similar experience of trafficking, paired with similarities in the political, economic, and social post-socialist developments. Despite the differences among the conditions of Croatia, Serbia, and Bulgaria in the last two decades—differences due to the violent collapse of Yugoslavia and the creation of independent states, as well as the relatively peaceful transition to democracy in Bulgaria—the three films share common perceptions of local people, their economic circumstances and their ethics. And to caution again, the acknowledgment of commonalities cannot obscure the observation of differences in the ways these films depict trafficking, perpetrators, and victims.

Instead of studying these films in the context of their national cinemas and their representation of women, crime, and trauma, I center on the portrayal of the trafficking story. I have to stress that *The Melon Route* is not only a trafficking film, but painstakingly explores the humanity of a former soldier and outcast-turned-criminal while depicting the story of Chinese people smuggled and/or trafficked from Bosnia and Herzegovina to Croatia. In light of the 2015–2016 refugee crisis in Europe and the Balkans, it is important to examine the similarities and differences in the legal definitions of smuggling and trafficking.

The definition of trafficking in human beings is outlined in the Palermo Protocol and in the United Nations' "Protocol against the Smuggling of Migrants by Land, Sea and Air" from 2000 (the so-called Smuggling of Migrants Protocol), which, like the Palermo Protocol, supplements the United Nations Convention against Transnational Organized Crime. According to article 3(a) of the protocol, "Smuggling of migrants" means "the procurement, in order to obtain, directly or indirectly, a financial or other material benefit, of the illegal entry of a person into a State Party of which the person is not a national or a permanent resident" (2000, 2). The protocol further defines "illegal entry" as "crossing borders without complying with the necessary requirements for legal entry into the receiving State" (article 3b, 2000, 2). It becomes clear that while smuggling ends at the destination, trafficking does not, and trafficked persons are exploited after arrival and often during travel. Usually people who are smuggled have agreed to be illegally transported—that is, to be moved from one place to another—but the consent of trafficked persons is either non-existent or obtained through deceptive means. These distinctions are, however, challenged by the observed reality. The "illegal status [of smuggled persons] puts them at the mercy of their smugglers, who often force the migrants to work for years in the illegal labour market to pay off the debts incurred as a result of their transportation" (Dinan 2008, 75).

The European Union Agency for Fundamental Rights states that victims of labor exploitation who are illegal migrants are often reluctant to report the exploitation to authorities, out of "fear of arrest, detention and deportation or expulsion" (FRA 2015, 79). To report the latest refugee crisis and mass migration towards Europe, media stories use the terms "smuggling" and "trafficking" interchangeably and incorrectly. It is worthwhile to re-think their differences based on definitions, and focus on elaborating effective prevention, penalty, and victim support measures for both.

Although *The Melon Route* was produced in 2006, prior to the recent migrant and refugee movements in the Balkans, this clarification is warranted because the film exposes a case in which a smuggled individual becomes a trafficked person experiencing abuse. It tells the story of a young Chinese woman who, together with her father and several other Chinese people, has taken the dangerous path of illegally traveling through the Balkans in an attempt to reach Germany. A criminal gang of smugglers transports them by minivan to the bank of the river Sava, which marks the border between Bosnia and Herzegovina and Croatia. There, with force, they employ the services of a local recluse, Mirko (Krešimir Mikić), who is supposed to deliver them through to the other bank of the Sava into Croatia. Impatient to receive his payment for the transportation from an older Chinese man, the leader of the gang, Seki (Leon Lucev), brutally grabs all of the old man's money at gunpoint and leaves them with Mirko—a first sign of the abuse smuggled people can endure.

Although brief, the scene clearly depicts the aggression and cruelty of the local gang and the mistreatment that the smuggled Chinese people face. In Plate 21, while the man's face (soon the viewer learns that he is the young woman's father) reveals his bewilderment, the woman's (Mei Sun) horrified expression foreshadows the group's destiny and her traumatic experience. In the middle of a foggy night, Mirko loads them on a small dinghy that before long begins to sink, and they all drown, except Mirko, who also saves the young Chinese woman. In a short exchange between Mirko and Seki while still on the bank, Mirko warns Seki that the boat leaks, but Seki, expressing a total lack of concern, orders Mirko to proceed. In the first seven or eight minutes of the film, the viewer is already introduced to Mirko, depicted as a former soldier, loner, and addict who lives in an isolated decrepit house on the bank of the Sava away from town—an outcast whose early actions in the film define him as a criminal. A more perceptive viewer, however, notices that the camera introduces Mirko by attentively focusing on him in bed in his bare and rundown room, lingering on his body and his unsteady movements getting out of bed. Although the overall portrayal of him and his environment is depressing and even repulsive, the attention the director pays to him and minor but important details like the two crosses hanging on the wall above his bed (Plate 22) hint that these first impressions about him may be deceptive. He develops into a more complex character than this introduction suggests.

The remaining 120 minutes of the film tell the story of the Chinese woman's desperation at having lost her father and finding herself with no money, no language to communicate in a foreign country, sought by criminals, and at the mercy of Mirko. Their relationship slowly evolves from total miscomprehension and aggression to puzzlement and more humane interactions, and even to tenderness and love. The power of the film lies in the depiction of the woman's traumatic experience, as well as Mirko's transformation from a pariah with a questionable moral horizon to a person who exhibits compassion for another human being's suffering, forced by circumstances to kill in order to protect the Chinese woman and help her pursue her dream. Emotional scenes showing the woman seeking her father after the boat sank, as well as her struggle to survive in and around Mirko's house move the viewer and expose the overlapping conditions of smuggled and trafficked people. Without intruding on her pain and avoiding too many close-ups, the camera gently follows her, allowing the viewer to relate and identify with her pain. In intriguing narrative twists and turns, the gang begins to harass Mirko and his younger friend in attempts to find the girl. After they succeed, they lock her in a basement and abuse her. This violence, however, does not quench their thirst and they beat up Mirko's friend, disposing of his half-conscious body on Mirko's pier. The camera centers on Mirko's face, revealing profound frustration and desperation. While avoiding focusing too closely on the Chinese woman's face, the camera often considerately examines Mirko's face in frontal close-ups, revealing his disturbance and psychological transformation. Forced by the complete corruption and failure of state and local institutions that are supposed to maintain law and order, in a violent and gruesome scene Mirko kills the thugs and their boss (an established local businessman). He frees the Chinese woman and helps her and his friend to leave Bosnia and Herzegovina and head to Germany.

A psychological drama, *The Melon Route* investigates both the human ability for compassion in marginalized individuals and the

Human trafficking survivor who smashed triathlon world record

By **Leif Coorlim, CNN**

Updated 12:39 PM ET, Tue May 17, 2016

CNN report on survivor

Image of slave ship in Al Jazeera's *Slavery: A 21st Century Evil*

Gang leader holds smuggled persons at gunpoint (*The Melon Route*)

Two crosses hang above Mirko's bed (*The Melon Route*)

Pimp threatens trafficked sisters (*Sisters*)

Sisters physically abused and "broken" (*Sisters*)

Samy's gaze focused on conditions of Bulgarian Roma (*Face Down*)

Samy's gaze fixated on living standards of minority (*Face Down*)

Mother scolds her daughter for returning home (*Face Down*)

ASTRA's interactive website "Prevent, Protect, Compensate"

Balkans ACT Now mobile application

ASTRA poster puts perpetrators' bodies on display

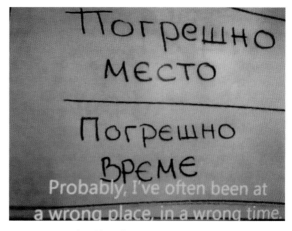

"The Bloody Penny" animation

"The Bloody Penny" dismembered doll

Animus rotten fruit posters

banality of evil, Hannah Arendt's concept that will be discussed in more detail in the next chapter. As a former soldier, Mirko is no doubt affected by the traumas of the war, and exhibits signs of posttraumatic stress disorder with his detachment from life and community. The banality of evil is portrayed permeating human relations. While one of the opening scenes shows from a distance an excavation of a mass grave (a reminder of the atrocities of the war), criminal activities and the abuse of human rights and human lives persist as if society has learned nothing from its recent past. Mirko, the outcast, behaves more humanely than the ordinary inhabitants of a town, from the policeman to the thugs and their boss. While the boss is often depicted in his daily routine of inspecting his business operations and tending to his family, he is also shown to have no scruples when it comes to his disregard of human lives.

Post-Yugoslav conditions in Bosnia and Herzegovina and its struggles to find resolutions for its divided society notwithstanding, this film looks deeply into the society's broken social structures and human links. Directed by the Croatian filmmaker Branko Schmidt and produced in Croatia, it portrays a small community on the Bosnian and Herzegovinian bank of the Sava, and one can argue that instead of focusing on its own society's problems, the film explores the consequences of the war and the transition to democracy on the other side of the border. It is different from Western films, which project their anxieties for superiority on East Europeans seen as either victims or criminals and depict Westerners as rescuers. In *The Melon Route*, there is neither hope for restored social relations, nor positive heroes. The only myth that the film possibly perpetuates with its ending is the solution of the moral crisis sought in the West. Although Mirko's young friend and the Chinese woman depart for Germany, the desperation and gloominess with which the society is presented do not leave room for optimism, especially because Mirko sends them away while he stays behind. As Anja Šošić concludes her review of the film: "The film is a closed circle and ends where it began, only Mirko's hands are stained with blood. He saved someone but salvation is denied to him" (2009).[1] In the overall overcast, dim,

---

[1] "Filmska je zagrada zatvorena, kraj je poput početka, samo je Mirko sada uprljan krvlju. Spasio je nekoga, no njemu samu spasenje ostaje uskraćeno." The translations of all East European sources and films are by the author, unless otherwise stated.

and rainy atmosphere of the film, the light bulb in Mirko's room often flickers in the dark, reinforcing the impression of Mirko's humane gestures interwoven with brutality and murders.

Unlike *The Melon Route*, which focuses mostly on the psychological and social effects of the Yugoslav war while depicting a smuggling and trafficking story, the Serbian film *Sisters* centers entirely on a trafficking case, from the recruitment of young Serbian women to their exploitation, being forced to provide sexual services, and their trauma and survival. Produced by a Serbian independent film company but supported by the International Organization of Migration (IOM) as well as the European Union through the competition "Media Support in the Sphere of European Integration" (Podrška medijima u oblasti evropskih integracija), the film portrays both the perpetrators and the trafficked women as part of Serbian society.

Screened in Serbia on both the big screen and on television (Channel 1) and with a cast of young, unknown actresses and actors, the film's objective is clearly educational. Two women, the 23-year-old Maria (Ivana Vuković) and her younger sister Katarini (Ana Maljević) excitedly inform their mother and grandfather that after responding to a newspaper advertisement, they were selected for jobs in Italy. While the mother shares their excitement and is supportive, the grandfather doubts this prospect, but in the end consents. This scene hints at the economic hardship of the family and lack of opportunities for the young women. The viewer sees the two sisters happily entering the van of their employer and soon realizes that they are being transported to a brothel. It is worth mentioning that while the detail that the brothel is in Serbia is shared with the viewer, Maria, Katarini, and three more women believe that they are in Italy. This element is unusual for feature films and most documentaries, which trace trafficking across borders and ignore domestic trafficking, for it is less sensational and perhaps more troublesome for viewers. The subsequent scenes depict the ways in which pimps "break" the trafficked women through psychological threats, drugs, and violence (Plates 23 and 24). The viewer follows the traumatic journey of the two girls who first object, struggle, and finally succumb to the abuse, begin to obey, and provide sexual services to clients of the brothel. A few scenes focus on the women's living conditions, sharing a locked room in which they are kept only in their underwear.

In another unusual narrative element avoided by other films, *Sisters* explores the different psychological reactions of Maria and Katarini.[2] After the pimp begins to favor Katarini and offer her small gestures of kindness, she slowly dissociates from the other women and her sister and identifies with him and the other men and women controlling the brothel. Her Stockholm syndrome is a reaction studied and recorded in cases of trafficking, but other films prefer to depict a more stereotypical victimhood. In a similar attempt to expose less-featured elements of trafficking, *Sisters* also shows that the traffickers are not exclusively men—a documented fact (Hopkins and Nijboer 2004). Although the Frontline documentary *Sex Slaves* also indicated that women are involved as pimps, overall filmmakers opt to represent mostly men as perpetrators.

Following the trafficking story, the film presents Maria's escape and the help that she receives from a local psychologist and the police. The process of coming to terms with what has happened to her, her trauma, and her drug addiction, although briefly, are depicted as difficult steps in her recovery. A drawback in the narrative is that it fails to explore in depth her post-trafficking journey, as her addiction, for example, is shown in only one scene, after which she somewhat miraculously functions well. The last episodes of the film depict the judicial process and expose the imperfect anti-trafficking legislation, which requires survivors to face their abusers in court. While Maria and the other three rescued women, despite their emotional difficulties, identify their pimp and narrate their abuse, Katarini refuses to do so. The pimp demands that she look him in the eye while confirming his story that the women were not forced to prostitute, but did this on their own accord. After a brief emotional conflict, Katarini claims that she was not a whore but ran the PR side of the brothel.[3] The film ends with Maria at home looking for a job, while a brief scene shows Katarini sold to other traffickers.

Although with modest aesthetic qualities compared to *The Melon Route*, *Sisters* appears to present the trafficking story more or less accu-

---

[2] *Sex Traffic* to a lesser extend also presents the two sisters' different reactions.
[3] For discussion on the detrimental effects of this judicial process on the survivors, see the M.A. thesis of Sophia Papadimos, "Human Trafficking in Serbia and Greece: a Comparative Analysis of a Victim-Centered Approach."

rately, including a few aspects that other films ignore. More importantly for my argument, both perpetrators and trafficked people are Serbian and the case is one of domestic trafficking. Unlike Western productions, this film is not interested in focusing on the West as the demand side of trafficking, but explores the perils of its own society. As also observed in *The Melon Route*, these filmmakers pose pertinent questions about the social conditions and moral values of their societies, resulting from both the Yugoslav war and the transition to free-market economy and democracy.

At the same time, there are certain stereotypes that the film perpetuates. Studying the anti-trafficking videos and other print materials produced by IOM in Eastern Europe, Rutvica Andrijašević calls attention to the simplistic presentations of victims and perpetrators in these materials:

> In La Strada/IOM campaign, the reader is told that young women have been deceived by agencies or individuals and then coerced into prostitution abroad. The representation of trafficking relies on an extremely simplistic dualism that sets apart young and innocent victims from malevolent traffickers who lure them into migrating abroad. To put it differently, within the discursive economy of trafficking the narrative of women's victimhood is interwoven and contingent upon the narrative of criminality (2007, 32).

While *Sisters* suffers from a similar simplification—with the incursion of women among the traffickers, the Stockholm syndrome, and the presentation of the trafficking case entirely in Serbia—it attempts to use details that rarely appeal to other filmmakers and indicate the complexities of trafficking. It is interesting to note that viewers' online responses express approval of the film and its educational and informative effectiveness and advocate for its screening (Prvi i najveći ženski 2011).

Even more unusual but also more problematic in its depiction of a trafficking case is the Bulgarian-French production *Face Down*. The film tells the story of a French criminal, Samy (Melvil Poupaud), who is involved with a Bulgarian criminal organization that smuggles counterfeit euros from Bulgaria to France. Caught by the French police, in order to avoid jail time he agrees to work with them and infiltrate a Bulgarian trafficking ring. After attempting to get close to a Bulgarian trafficked woman, Elka (Seher Nebieva), who is working as prostitute in France and failing, Samy forces her to join him in his return to Bulgaria. There, he intends to buy women and traffic them to France, following his undercover task to reach the ringleader who resides in Vienna. Caught between the demands of his counterfeit currency associates and the French police, he has little chances of succeeding in his goal. While in Bulgaria, Elka takes him to her family and to the local ringleader, a woman—all of whom are ethnic Bulgarian Roma. As it becomes clear that Elka's mother has sold her and scolds her for returning in fear that the criminals will want their money back, the horrific living and social conditions of the Bulgarian minority are exposed harshly (Plates 25, 26, and 27).

While this depiction reveals the subhuman living standards of Roma minorities in Bulgaria, it hides the Westerner's fascination or repulsion with this social reality. Since the camera is aligned with Samy's point of view when he and Elka approach her neighborhood, as it becomes obvious from the three screenshots, the viewer notices how Samy's gaze is drawn to the side-of-the-road makeshift dwellings (Plate 25). Romani life is entirely presented through Samy's view. When one adds to this the construction of the opening scene of the film, which shows live bar musicians singing what is known in Bulgaria as "chalga" genre—primitive and sexist lyrics accompanied by music influenced by Romani and folklore rhythms—the whole presentation of Bulgarian reality becomes subordinated to kitsch culture, criminals, and families willing to sell their daughters. While such cases are recorded in Bulgaria, detailing only such a case presents a one-sided picture of trafficking in Bulgaria and its social conditions.[4] In addition to these nar-

---

[4] The Animus Association Foundation worked with and archived a similar case, in which a girl was sold into marriage and moved to the Netherlands with her husband, who forced her into prostitution. When she became pregnant, she was abandoned on the streets and returned to Bulgaria. Her recovery and re-integration into society was difficult because she was a minor and taking her back to her family was not an option. The information was presented by Maria Tchomarova at the conference "The Dark Side of Globalization: Trafficking in People," which I organized at the Ohio State University in 2004. I would like to thank all participants for their presentations and active discussion, from which I learned a lot.

rative and cinematic flaws, Samy, similar to Mirko, begins to relate to Elka and sympathize with her situation. He decides to free her from her pimps, thus disobeying both the French police and his own gang boss. While Mirko's transformation is portrayed as more human compared to the behavior of the other local characters, in *Face Down*, Samy, the Frenchman, is capable of compassion, but all the Bulgarian characters are irredeemable. This impression is cemented by the film's ending, in which Elka betrays Samy and returns to her family and her pimps. This ending certainly offers no hope for Bulgarian Roma, but also indicates that their conditions of social and economic marginalization and depression provide no exit.

In the online Bulgarian magazine *12*, journalist Elitsa Mateeva noted that the film has strong qualities, like projecting powerful emotions. But she also acknowledged that certain narrative aspects could have been developed better. "I experienced the film as if something was missing, as if there was a compromise."[5] Rightly so, she identifies the compromise in the nature of the co-production. The young director Kamen Kalev, educated in France, sought co-producers for his first two films and secured them in Sweden. For *Face Down*, he received funding from France but on one condition: interviewed by Mateeva, his cameraman Iulian Atanasov clarifies the demand of the French producers. "The only condition," he said, "was that the predominant language had to be French and we were very meticulous during the editing to meet the requirement of the producers" (Mateeva 2015). In my view, Kalev not only met the demands of the French producers, but exceeded them with the presentation of Bulgarian reality without salvation through the depressed and neglected Roma communities and the French character's reborn morality.

Tomislav Longinović and Roumiana Deltcheva address this intriguing response of East Europeans who, in a cultural production, answer to stereotypical Western constructions of the Balkans with "an

---

[5] "S litse nadolu" bezsporno pritezhava kachestva, no mi se struva, che niakoi linii v siuzheta mozheha da se izvedat i po-dobre. Prizheviavah filma s chustvoto, che neshto lipsva, che siakash e napraven kompromis. (*Face Down* undoubtedly has [good] qualities but I have a feeling that some narrative lines can be developed better. I experienced the film as if something was missing, as if there was a compromise.)

internalized culture of 'self-Balkanization'" (Longinović) or by per-petuating the "misperceptions" themselves (Deltcheva). "While suc-cumbing to a stereotype may range from innocently misleading to blatantly manipulative, it also reinforces the dangerous theme of the victim as poor, illiterate, downtrodden, and ultimately marginalized" (Deltcheva 2005, 208–209). In the case of Kalev, one can also argue that in addition to the demands he had to meet from the French pro-ducer, his Western education influenced his view of his native coun-try's condition.

Another problematic aspect of the film lies in its blurred depic-tion of the conditions of trafficking and prostitution. Some of the media commentaries on the film after its opening in the fall of 2015 reflect that confusion. In *Vesti.bg*, Monika Poncheva states that the film addresses a "problem painful for Bulgarians—trafficking in people" (2015).[6] A bit later, however, she describes Elka as a prostitute, not a trafficked woman.

This critique should not invalidate some of the successful quali-ties of the film. Although presented as the demand side of trafficking, France is not the focus of the film, which painfully (even too painfully, as discussed above) focuses on the destruction of human values in Bul-garian society. Kalev's choice to work with non-professional actors in every role except Samy projects truthfulness and creates a documen-tary feel.

Although very different in their aesthetics and narrative structures, the three films discussed here share a few commonalities. They all examine trafficking in the context of the collapsed moral foundation and economic conditions of their societies and do not seek to project the blame onto others, especially the West. The perpetrators and the trafficked women are all members of their own communities, except the Chinese woman in *The Melon Route*, as the existence of trafficking is fueled in each case by economic depravity and, more significantly,

---

[6] "Delo na rezhisiora na "Iztochni piesi" i "Ostrovut" i nezavisimata produ-tsenska kompaniia Waterfront Film, lentata zasiaga nabolial za bulgarskata realnost problem – trafikyt na hora." (A product of the director of Eastern Plays and The Island and the independent production company WF, the film concerns a problem painful for Bulgarian reality—trafficking in people.)

by corruption and moral decay. In addition, none of these films shows a happy ending or proffers any hope. These shared positions present a significant shift from the Western productions examined in the previous chapter.

It is important to elaborate here that while most of the Western films uncover the social conditions of Eastern Europe that might appear similar to the ones portrayed in the Balkan films, they often gaze at these communities, objectifying them while presenting the West in a more positive light—often through the triumphs of their forces which combat trafficking, assist victims, and break criminal rings. Even more troubling, these films never focus on cases of domestic trafficking, including perpetrators and victims, i.e. members of their own societies. Unlike Western filmmakers and producers, these Balkan film directors do not present a binary picture of the world seeking to project blame. They are concerned with their own societies and their struggles to overcome various challenges resulting from their countries' transitions to democracy. It appears that these Balkan directors, although successful in different degrees, all attempt to look deeply into their own cultures and communities instead of gazing at others.

NGO Anti-Trafficking Media Materials

Examining Slovenian print media (daily newspapers and magazines from January 2001 to May 2004) reporting on trafficking, Mojca Pajnik finds that the media coverage varies from claiming that trafficking in Slovenia does not exist, labeling trafficked women as naïve and prostitutes, to depicting policemen as "models of good behavior" who free and save women and imprison the criminals (2004, 69). Studying in more detail the portrayal of trafficked women, Pajnik identifies four major frames of images: 1) "women are often photographed standing by the road. They wear short skirts and high heels and their images are often blurred"; 2) "women are photographed in front of buildings"; 3) photos show "a woman's figure outlined in a dark room"; and 4) "women are photographed while dancing in either underwear or dancing costumes" (71). Concluding her study, Pajnik points out several problems: "One-sidedness, vagueness, simplification, stereotyping—these are common media strategies in addressing trafficking"

(72). Even more ineffective is media's "depicting women as prostitutes" and "reducing trafficking to police business" (71).

Similarly critical of the constructions of women in trafficking situations, as well as doubtful about their effectiveness is Andrijašević in her analysis of IOM anti-trafficking visual materials and videos produced in Eastern Europe, in some cases by LaStrada network organizations. She writes:

> [I]t is quite difficult to conclude that IOM's counter-trafficking campaigns empower women. The images here discussed do not re-signify dominant representational practices nor do they propose new forms of representation for women. Quite the contrary, they deploy techniques that frame women's body in a voyeuristic manner and lock it into an (im)position of immobility. In this way, the IOM's campaigns convey images of unhappy, desperate and suicidal women, and consequently re-install the stereotypical rendering of feminine bodies in terms of passive objects of violence. Moreover, by highlighting the innocence and unwillingness of these young white female bodies, the IOM's campaigns re-propose the conventional trafficking rhetoric. This rhetoric, as Jo Doezema (1992: 2) has shown in her analysis of trafficking in women's media imaginary, is centred upon "the paradigmatic image [...] of a young and naive innocent lured or deceived by evil traffickers into a life of sordid horror from which escape is nearly impossible" (2007, 41–42).

While I concur with her general findings, it is important to stress that all campaign materials that Andrijašević examined are produced and/ or created by IOM. As it becomes clear in Andrijašević's analysis, they do not depart from the Western ideology of viewing trafficked women. As mentioned in Chapter 3, Hesford similarly critiques the Bulgarian video *Open Your Eyes* produced by IOM.

While I believe that the above analysis convincingly exposes media's and NGOs' flaws in the materials they produce, I examine a few NGO animated videos and other prevention materials from ASTRA, Belgrade, Open Gate, Skopje, and Animus, Sofia, which reveal attempts to move away from the above patterns of mostly ineffective trafficking depictions. As stated on its website, ASTRA was founded in 2000 and is "dedicated to the eradication of all forms of trafficking in human beings, especially in women and children."[7] ASTRA's website offers their latest video and interactive web animation named "Prevent, Protect, Compensate." The material is produced with the support of numerous organizations from the EU and the Western Balkans. It is created as part of a project called "Balkans ACT Now," as ACT stands for Against Crime of Trafficking. Several NGOs participate in it, including ASTRA and Open Gate as well as EU institutions like The Netherlands Helsinki Committee and the French Ministry of Justice. The two versions (video and website) contain the same narrative and information, but while one is a one-minute video clip, the interactive website presents a static drawing of a sad young woman, Hana, sitting on a bench, looking straight at the viewer (Plate 28). It directs Internet users to scroll down, and the narrative in six languages (Bosnian, Croatian, Macedonian, Montenegrin, Serbian, and English) succinctly tells a simple story of hope, deceit, capture by police, and court procedures which, the narrative stresses, have continued for seven years while Hana has no support. While the case of trafficking is told with brief sentences and the web user is asked to scroll down after each sentence, the emphasis is on the inadequate legal system and the lack of compensation for the trafficked woman. The video clip shows the same, but with an animation depicting a city skyline, Hana in a room with bare furnishing, a shadow of a man at the door with a lifted arm threatening violence, a police raid, and Hana testifying in court. These quick scenes alternate up to the middle of the clip, and the rest focuses on Hana's face, with a voice-over narrating the rights that a survivor should have and the compensation that she should receive. Despite the fact that the video includes the presence of the sad (and some might conclude, victimized) woman, in my view the authors succeed in avoiding any objectification of the woman's body. They are not interested that much in the story of trafficking, but in the rehabilitation and the human rights of the trafficked woman.

Even more appealing to young people whom Balkans ACT Now attempts to reach is the mobile application ACT has created. It contains several functions: a game, a trafficking facts sheet, and a quiz. It

---

[7] I visited ASTRA only once in the summer of 2013 and my knowledge of their work is limited compared to my familiarity with Open Gate and Animus.

is available in all of the official languages of the countries in former Yugoslavia plus English, French, Dutch, and Russian. Fun to play, the game and the quiz provide accurate information targeting and deconstructing existing myths about trafficking. In the game, users can choose from six young characters (three women and three men) and proceed through various scenarios of trafficking (Plate 29). The game offers possible options and asks the user to make choices that lead to different trafficking situations. At the end of each character's storyline, the application includes important facts and accurate information. The multiple-choice quiz similarly engages the users and repudiates all myths surrounding trafficking. For example, to the question, "[What happens] when victims escape the trafficking rings?" there are three possible answers: 1) They recover quickly and go on to live a normal life; 2) They receive a lot of money once their trafficker is convicted; and 3) It all depends on the support they receive. If there is no one to help them, there is a risk that they will find themselves in a similar situation again. Or, to the question, "Where does human trafficking take place?" the answers are: 1) In brothels and nightclubs; 2) In the street, in private apartments, on construction sites, on agricultural estates, in factories. In any place that could enable traffickers to make profits by exploiting people; and 3) In poor, dangerous, and criminalized neighborhoods. If a wrong answer is selected, the next screen explains the mistake and offers more options. Undoubtedly, the application is an effective educational and preventive tool designed to reach young people, but is also crafted with care to avoid stereotypes and teach the facts about trafficking.

In addition, ASTRA uses a poster that exposes the torsos of naked men, obviously perpetrators (Plate 30). It provides the hotline telephone number of ASTRA with a narrative stating that women are not meat and children are not slaves. Under the link "education and prevention" on ASTRA's website, the organization states that its visual material purposefully avoids the portrayal of any female image and centers instead on the abusers.

The same tendencies can be observed in the video materials that Open Gate posted on its website. Three short video animations deserve attention. "Maria and the Ideal Lover," ranked the best multi-media anti-trafficking product by Internet users, is perhaps the least effective because of its suggestion that a woman can be easily deceived (La-

Strada). As the title reveals, it presents a charming man and attentive lover with whom Maria quickly falls in love, to be locked, abused, and sold by him to other traffickers. The three-minute animation is interlaced by narrative warnings, which appear in the form of typed paper clippings that say: "Watch it! Maria's story can be yours!" At the end, the video suggests an alternative scenario in which Maria rejects the advances of the "ideal lover" and safely goes home. Most interesting in this video is not the blame cast upon the woman (a repeated approach in media), but the fact that an online audience ranked this particular project, created by students from a community college in the city of Shtip, the best. Undoubtedly, the recognition that it received reveals that attitudes blaming the woman's naïveté (Maria falls in love quickly and follows her lover without much thought or consideration) still persist among Macedonian web users.

More effective is another Open Gate video material, voted the best by a jury of experts (LaStrada). The powerful and creative animation by Angela Chaloska, called "The Bloody Penny," tells the story of a penny changing hands, and through its journey the artist presents various trafficking scenarios visually conveyed by simple drawings. Lasting 4.25 minutes, the clip repeatedly uses the "explanation" for all trafficking cases being: "Wrong place, wrong time" (Plate 31). The stories of child labor exploitation in a doll factory, a child beggar, and a sex-trafficked woman end with a voice-over informing the viewer that these people have their stories, but nobody cares to hear them— rather, the reply or explanation is always "wrong place, wrong time." Repudiating this "justification" of the existence of trafficking, the artist states at the end that all these destinies are the result of human trafficking and the voice-over assumes a first-person position declaring individuality and independence ("I am not a marionette and I want to control my own destiny"). The video integrates imaginative black-and-white pencil drawings, which do not simply illustrate the narrative, but suggest other meanings and offer additional information.

Various body (doll) pieces on the table present an impaired childhood experience resulting from child labor (Plate 32). Other drawings contain only question marks or crossed-out human figures, which, paired with the voice-over interrogating the reasons for trafficking, create a more engaging educational film that demands a more attentive viewer. Inspiring and different from other video prevention materials, which appear simplistic and shallow, "The Bloody Penny" rightly deserves the high praise given to its creator by peers.

Supported by the Macedonian government, the British Embassy in Skopje, and LaStrada, Amsterdam, Open Gate uses also three short (25 seconds) educational clips. Each clip presents an animated story of a trafficked person: a man deceived through an "employment agency" and exploited in the construction industry; a woman responding to an ad and also exploited but rescued; and a child sold by his father and forced to work under inhumane conditions. Each of these clips end with Open Gate's hotline telephone number and a title, "Raise your voice against trafficking in people." The simplistic presentation of familiar scenarios notwithstanding, these three clips are constructive for their avoidance of sex trafficking and in their focused message aiming to call attention to the problem and advertise the NGO's services. As mentioned earlier, film and video materials of sex trafficking appeal to filmmakers and producers and are used in campaigns against human trafficking in general, because "sex sells" and because crimes of sexual nature evoke a higher degree of empathy.

The materials provided by ASTRA and Open Gate obviously differ from the ones analyzed and criticized by Pajnik and Andrijašević. The video clips and the mobile application discussed address and deconstruct myths about trafficking by presenting accurate information in an artistic form attractive to youth, avoid (in most cases) the objectification of women's bodies, and attempt to empower young people by educating them about their rights and their options. Focusing on La-Strada/IOM produced materials in The Czech Republic, Ukraine, and Moldova, Andrijašević insists that "[s]ince all the available migration venues lead into coerced prostitution, the campaign implies that the safest option is to remain home" (2007, 31). These findings, however, do not appear to accurately describe other (and more recent) prevention campaign materials from the Balkans, although both Open Gate and Animus belong to the LaStrada network.

The materials used by Animus are both original and different from the posters critiqued by Andrijašević. They aim to instruct young people by offering information in ways that can reach them, such as flash drives on silicon bracelets handed out in schools or beermats distributed in bars, both with bare facts about trafficking and a hotline telephone number. More interesting are four advertisement posters commissioned by Animus (Plates 33–36). They aim to expose deceitful job offers and urge people to think about the information provided in them. Visually, they present a photograph of a rotten fruit—a brown overripe banana, a half-eaten and dried-up apple, a moldy orange, and spoiled strawberries—on different color backgrounds: light green, yellow, blue, and pink. Text in the upper left corner in large font simply states in Bulgarian: "Banana picking 450 euros a week" or "Strawberry picking 600 [British] pounds a week." On the opposite bottom right corner, it reads: "If you smell something rotten in such ads, call 02/981 76 86." The posters are not only aesthetically appealing, but catch attention with their novel and provocative combination of visual and print elements that contain unusual and conflicting information intended to make the viewer think more about what s/he sees and reads. Added to this is a humorous link between the images of rotten fruit and the text "if you smell something rotten, call…" which works only in Bulgarian, for in English the phrase translates in "if you smell something fishy…" Unlike the media coverage and campaign series discussed by Pajnik and Andrijašević, these posters do not focus on women as victims and do not suggest that the safest option is staying home. They only urge people to read job postings critically, and thus empower them.

Overall, the three feature films from the Balkans discussed here differ considerably from Western films in their construction of the trafficking actors: perpetrators, victims/survivors, and rescuers. The Balkan films are unlike Western productions, which mostly create a black-and-white presentation of the trafficking process, identifying criminals and victims as Eastern European and rescuers as Western, elevating the status of the West as the morally just protector, perpetuating not only stereotypes about trafficking but ineffectively informing policy makers, who often prefer to focus on the criminalization and international security side of trafficking while ignoring the economic and human rights aspects. The Balkan productions reveal concerns with the moral and economic collapse of their own communities and depict much more complex trafficking situations, exposing local conditions that should inform government agencies and policy makers. This is not to say that they are all equally effective in their attempts, but the filmmakers are clearly motivated by other factors compared to their Western counterparts.

The materials included in the prevention campaigns of ASTRA, Open Gate (except "The Ideal Lover" video), and Animus attempt to refocus efforts and the attention of their audiences from sex trafficking to all forms of trafficking, including that of men and children for labor exploitation. Clearly, these NGOs understand that criminals take advantage of people's desire for employment and better lives, a fact that is often overlooked in Western media products opting to focus on sex trafficking, the naïveté of women not interested in the possible reasons for it, and the brutality of perpetrators. While some are more successful than others, the campaign materials aim to shift public and government efforts from tendencies to discourage people from pursuing their dreams, to better educating them and empowering them. While these are just a few case studies, they still show the shifting efforts of NGOs.

CHAPTER 6

Trauma: Screening Violence and the "Viewer-Witness"

An additional and no less important aspect of the films and media products that I discussed in the two previous chapters is their effectiveness and ability to shock the viewer and create a citizen who is ready to take action against trafficking. One possible way to examine this is to study the representation of trauma in relation to the spectator. The representation of trafficking trauma necessitates a complex analysis and understanding, for it hides latent conflicts between evoking empathy and inciting titillation and disbelief. This chapter addresses the following questions: 1) Are images of raped and violated bodies traumatic per se? 2) Do they require background knowledge and cultural translation? 3) How do films exploring the trauma of sex trafficking create vicarious trauma and does this facilitate or interfere with activism and pro-social cultural change?

I examine representative traumatic scenes from three types of cinematic productions: Western, East European, and co-productions of Western and East European partners. To the first group (US and Western) belong *Human Trafficking*, *Lilya 4-ever*, and *Promised Land* (2004, Israel/France); to the second (East European), *Lady Zee* and *You Are Alive*; and to the third, *Svetlana's Journey* (2004, US/Bulgaria).

As it becomes clear from the information about the production of these films, a few of them are co-productions. In most cases, two Western European countries—or in the case of *Promised Land,* Israel and France—funded the films. Only *Svetlana's Journey* is co-produced by Western and East European parties. This classification matters because, as argued already, the producers cater to their own expectations and market demands, which often negatively affects the impact of these films on anti-trafficking campaigns.

This statement is not a new discovery in cinema and media studies, which for decades has been examining the agendas of Hollywood studios or the participation of the viewer in the creation of meaning.[1] For films on the subject of trafficking, however, this matters more because it leads to ineffective awareness campaigns and policies. In this chapter, I argue that the representation of trauma and its effectiveness can also be transformed and swayed by the cultural and gender backgrounds of both producers and viewers.

Vicarious Trauma and the Narrative

In *Moving People, Moving Images*, Brown theorizes at length about the possibility of making a trafficking film, of making visible what is invisible. "One wonders whether a film about human trafficking is possible, in perhaps the same way that a film about the Holocaust has, according to Jean-Luc Godard, similarly been impossible" (Brown et al. 2010, 47). While this debate, spearheaded by Cathy Caruth, emerged in academia in the early 1990s, Holocaust studies has developed further with the works of Dominick LaCapra and Joshua Hirsch. Trauma theory, as advanced by Caruth, Shoshana Felman, and Dori Laub, explores the paradoxical nature of traumatic memory and the crisis it generates for the traditional understanding of historical narratives, truth, and representation.

In addition, authors examine war films in relation to trauma and post-traumatic stress disorder. Most notably, Anton Kaes, in his work *Shell Shock Cinema*, traces decades of traumatic films: "[F]ilm noirs of the 1940s share with shell shock cinema of the 1920s a focus on psychologically troubled characters who have experienced something deeply disturbing in their past" (2009, 214). Pursuing a similar argument but investigating more recent media examples of trauma, the

---

[1] See, for example, Ray Pratt's *Projecting Paranoia* (2001), Stephen Prince's *Visions of Empire* (1992), and Robin Wood's *Hollywood from Vietnam to Reagan* (1986).

editors of *The Image and the Witness: Trauma, Memory, and Visual Culture* write:

> [A]rtists, filmmakers, photojournalists and amateurs continue to produce a vast body of images as a means to bear witness to historical trauma. It is not only images themselves, but also exciting curatorial and publicity initiatives such as exhibitions, public installations, film festivals, the World Wide Web, media activism and visual archives of past traumatic events which are now at the forefront of efforts to memorialize, interrogate and at times create the individual and collective experiences of these events. (Guerin and Hallas 2007, 5)

The function of cinema to reach the viewer by triggering traumatic memories or responses has been rather convincingly argued. Psychologists have established that therapists working with trauma survivors are often "vicariously" traumatized by the narratives they hear (Kaplan 2005). Film scholars, in turn, address the phenomenon of vicarious trauma in spectators. Hirsch reminds the reader of Susan Sontag's pioneering work on the effect of traumatic photographs on the viewer. About photographs of Bergen-Belsen and Dachau, Sontag writes: "Nothing I have seen—in photographs or in real life—ever cut me as sharply, deeply, instantaneously" (quoted in Hirsch 2009, 95). Hirsch, however, poses the question of cultural references: "There is no such thing as a traumatic image per se. But an image of atrocity may carry a traumatic potential, which, as it circulates among individuals and societies with common conceptual horizons, may be repeatedly realized in a variety of experiences of vicarious trauma" (Hirsch 2009, 98). Kaplan complicates the reception of traumatic images by introducing the concept of "empty" empathy: "Empathy elicited by images of suffering provided without any context or background knowledge" (2005, 93).

Often created with the intention of raising awareness, trafficking films and the bodily violations and traumatic images in them are expected to reach the viewer and create involved and proactive citizens. Hirsch and Kaplan argue that traumatic images do not per se produce an empathetic and witnessing spectator, as the scholars insist on "context" and "background knowledge" for the experience of vicarious trauma among viewers. To take these conditions into consideration, one ought to study the details of cultural context that these films offer—details that in turn relate to the spectator's "conceptual horizons."

A collection on trauma and cinema edited by Kaplan and Ban Wang proposes a framework for analysis of the spectator's involvement with the virtual nature of trauma. Kaplan and Wang outline four positions for viewers of trauma films: 1) "the position of being introduced to trauma through a film's themes and techniques, but where the film ends with a comforting 'cure'." 2) "the position of being vicariously traumatized." This position might have a negative effect as the vicarious trauma shocks the viewer and turns him or her away from the problem, or it might engage the viewer into wanting to know more and eventually do something. 3) "the position of being a voyeur," which usually involves a secret pleasure in exploiting the victims. 4) "the position of being a witness," which can open a space for "transformation of the viewer through empathic identification." This, they argue, is the most politically useful position (Kaplan and Wang 2009, 9–10). Hesford expands these positions, outlining modes of rhetorical witnessing. The most important are as follows: 1) the cultural, national, and transnational circulation, reception, and appropriation of testimonials; and 2) the methodological and ethical challenges posed by testimonials, called crisis of reference or crisis of witnessing (2004, 106). Hesford analyzes photography installations and documentaries that expose atrocities of the Yugoslav wars and especially war rapes.

While the above-mentioned concepts advanced by Kaplan, Wang, and Hirsch are utilized in this chapter to shed a better light on the effectiveness of traumatic trafficking films, I problematize these approaches as I also study the (unconscious) structures of political, cultural, and gender identities of producers and viewers. In doing so, I borrow from the argument and propositions of Allen Meek, who investigates Holocaust and 9/11 media representations and "stresses analysis of the unconscious structures of political identity rather than identification with, or empathy for, the victim/survivor of trauma" (2010, 1–2). Unlike Meek, however, who mostly develops "critical theory of historical trauma which allows us to understand human life subject to biopolitical power," (2010, 2) I pursue the efficacy of traumatic images of trafficking, not as a return of intrusive memories but as a motivating experience that can produce a socially engaged spectator. To that end, I investigate how media trafficking trauma works on viewers with different cultural and gender identities.

In *Human Trafficking*, the episodes of physical abuse depict young women who live in deplorable conditions. They are stripped, beaten, humiliated, insulted, threaten, and raped. Each of them must serve approximately twelve or thirteen "clients" every single day. The scene of rape and body violation of one of the Eastern European women is created through a quick montage of frames, presenting the whole or parts of the woman's horrified face and a man's body over her; a next scene shows her alone in a bathroom crying desperately and shaking.

Duguay's camera mixes sex, eroticism, and trauma.[2] When trafficked women are examined by their trafficker and potential clients, their bodies are exposed only in brassieres or undergarments with the camera presenting the point of view of the male protagonists. The camera (and the viewer's gaze) lingers on the women's figures, scrutinizing their bruised flesh. The camera, and through it the viewer, eroticizes the female body, thus enabling the spectator to assume "the position of being a voyeur." At the same time, the scenes of rape introduce a certain degree of shock. Through quick montage of her body parts and horrified facial expressions, the viewer is given the opportunity to sympathize with her and experience her horror (Plates 37 and 38). Whether this creates a "witness" rather than a voyeur is questionable. When one adds the happy ending or the "comforting cure," paired with the objectification of female bodies as well as the film's stereotypical presentations of East European women as naïve victims, I contend that *Human Trafficking* does not create an empathetic viewer.

In contrast to *Human Trafficking*, *Lilya 4-ever* allows for more sympathy and evokes the position of vicarious trauma. Director Lukas Moodysson shockingly presents the abuse, violence, and rape of Lilya while she is locked into a Swedish apartment. The film achieves a nauseating effect when viewers, after getting to know Lilya's character, observe her dreams morphing into nightmares. The scenes of abuse and rape, while detailed, are not the focus of the film. Nonetheless,

---

[2] I am grateful to Emily Schuckman-Matthews for her insights into the cinematic qualities of *Human Trafficking* and *Lilya 4-ever* and for the fruitful exchanges that we have had over the years.

two particular depictions of Lilya's bodily abuse are worth discussing. After she travels to Sweden and her trafficker picks her up, he locks her into an apartment and rapes her. This scene reveals her disbelief and terror at the turn of her fate. The perpetrator finds Lilya in the bathtub and violates her there. The physical violation happens off-screen: he enters the bathroom, closes the door and the camera remains focused on the door; the viewer hears her screaming "No, no, please no," and then noises of resistance, water, and fallen objects. In the next shot, the camera is positioned lower, showing Lilya looking distressed and despondent in the tub. The conscious decision of Moodysson to present her rape off-screen reveals his conviction not to play with or speculate on physical abuse on-screen and instead to attempt to achieve empathy by focusing on her distraught emotions after the fact.

Later, Lilya's numerous rapes are portrayed on-screen, but the director employs a technique that avoids her objectification. In these shots, the camera assumes her point of view and shows a series of men's repulsive faces and grotesque bodies, which dominate the screen (Plates 39, 40, and 41). Only the backgrounds of these violent interactions differ: from a bedroom, to the back of a store, to a sauna. By aligning the camera with Lilya's point of view, Moodysson invites the viewer to identify with her pain and to convey the hideousness of the men. Through this montage, the camera circumvents any eroticization of Lilya's body and projects only repugnance toward the violators.

Promised Land centers mainly on the inhumane conditions of trafficked Estonian women. They are smuggled through Egypt to be auctioned off as prostitutes in Israel. Truly international, the organized criminal ring includes Western Europeans, Russians, and Arabs. After humiliation and abuse, one of them manages to escape. Unlike any other film, *Promised Land* creates clear analogies between the Holocaust experience and the horror and violence of trafficking. A scene in which naked young women are being hosed down uncannily reminds the viewer of the Holocaust and the treatment of Jewish people in the camps.

The film graphically presents the rape of a young Estonian girl, a rape which occurs in the desert when the young women are being transported to Israel. With a documentary feel, it is shot in a closed frame with a handheld camera, creating very close proximity of the protagonists to the viewer. Extreme close-ups and an overused jittery camera style achieve an unsettlingly realistic presentation of the events with sickening effect (Plate 42). This style generates a ghastly reaction, as the spectator feels that s/he is being asked to participate in the violation. While this scene depicts the rape victim fully clothed and shows no flesh, subsequent episodes of the auctioning of the young women and their treatment in Israel expose their naked bodies.

The auction, however, is filmed very differently from the examination that the viewer witnesses in *Human Trafficking*. Director Amos Gitai uses a handheld camera and the dark of the desert night; the light comes only from a flashlight, which focuses mostly on the auctioned women's distraught faces, while their female boss, speaking in English, sells each one of them to the highest bidder in a group of Russian men. While three of the women are asked to lift their blouses and the flashlight shines on their breasts and once on a woman's buttocks, the jerky movements of the light paired with the handheld camera, which does not linger on the women's exposed flesh, do not allow the viewer much voyeuristic pleasure.

Similarly, when the women arrive in Israel and are placed on the ship "The Red Sea Star," they are asked to undress, keeping only their bikinis; then they are grouped together and showered with a hose. Captured with a full shot, the women are permitted to gather, mostly showing their backs to the men and the viewer. Through these techniques, Gitai achieves a balance between conveying their brutal victimization and avoiding eroticization of the young women's bodies.

The above discussion reveals that although all trafficking films that utilize shocking images attempt to evoke the spectator's empathy, not all of them are equally effective. Some, like *Human Trafficking*, achieve a voyeuristic position, as Kaplan and Wang define it, rather than a witnessing position that creates an empathetic viewer. Others, such as *Lilya 4-ever* and *Promised Land*, use techniques to avoid the objectification of women's bodies and attempt to focus instead on their trauma. The bodily violations depicted in the latter are likely to create a witnessing spectator who can vicariously feel the trauma of the trafficked women and is compelled to take action against trafficking. Such a viewer is capable of identifying with the abused person without casting blame on her for her condition.

Lady Zee (director Georgi Diulgerov), a Bulgarian production, portrays the hardship and lack of any meaningful future for a female orphan, Zlatina, who, approaching eighteen, is forced to leave the orphanage and start life on her own with neither family support nor any practical knowledge of the reality beyond the orphanage's walls. This film, unlike Western productions, which often suggest that women's naïveté might be the reason for their choices seeking better opportunities and falling victims of trafficking, pays special attention to the conditions of Bulgarian orphaned Roma, conditions that explain her choices in life. Zlatina's sexual awakening happens mid-narrative, and she sees selling her body as her only choice in life, for she knows nothing else. The viewer fully understands the decisions she makes and the lack of any other options in her life. Unsurprisingly, she transforms her appearance from a tomboy to an object of men's desire, doing so consciously in an attempt to control her life. Masquerading is her weapon vis-à-vis the world of male aggression.

Soon Zlatina (Lady Zee) engages in prostitution. Trying to take charge of her life, she ends up in Greece where she prostitutes under trafficking conditions; she is physically restrained and abused by her pimps. The traumatic scenes of her violation appear towards the end of the film. When her male friend from the orphanage, Lechko, locates her in a Greek brothel, the viewer, together with Lechko and a group of Greek men, watches her performing a cowgirl dance, topless. She first appears in a medium frontal shot, her entire upper body exposed and her head lowered. She walks and dances like she is drugged, and never looks up. The objectifying voyeurism powerfully defines her existence in the confined conditions of the brothel. In the next scene, Lechko is allowed to spend thirty minutes with her as a client. He is shocked to find her bruised physically and emotionally. Zlatina begs him to have sex with her; otherwise her pimps would beat her and take away her cigarettes, which she claims would crush her more than the beating. The scene continues to expose her naked torso and, while it is presented from Lechko's point-of-view, it is not a rape scene: Zlatina is on top and appears more embarrassed and detached than hurt as she looks aside, biting her lip (Plate 43). The next scene conveys her trauma more powerfully: a close-up of her face shows her quietly crying. Zlatina survives the hardship of her childhood and adolescence, showing little emotion. But now, when her dreams and life are crushed without hope, the viewer empathizes with her pain and emotional suffering.

Depiction of rape in *Human Trafficking*, horrified facial expression

Depiction of rape in *Human Trafficking*, focusing on horrified woman's eye

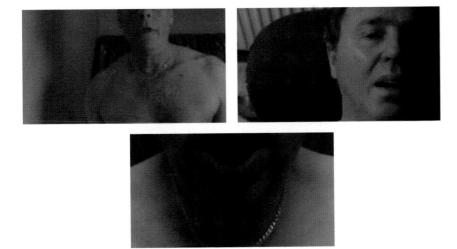

Grotesque bodies of male violators (*Lilya 4-ever*)

Promised Land rape scene

Zlatina biting lip (*Lady Zee*)

Crying, motionless face of rape victim (*You Are Alive*)

Pimp examines Svetlana's mouth in *Svetlana's Journey*

Animus poster of Anti-Trafficking Film Festival

One can safely argue that while Diulgerov reveals the voyeuristic objectification of Zlatina's body, he also focuses on her emotional trauma rather than on her physical abuse, a presentation that is more likely to evoke empathy and produce a "witnessing" spectator. Admittedly, the four positions outlined by Kaplan and Wang overlap, and it is difficult to establish with certainty which one most fittingly describes the spectator's engagement with films. Nonetheless, they can serve as a functional framework for the examination of the effectiveness of traumatic images.

The Macedonian film *You Are Alive* (discussed in Chapter 2) depicts the trafficking experience of two women, one middle-aged and the other a teenager. The film opens with a visibly abused and scared girl running through a dark park (with a handheld camera focused on her legs); when reaching a public phone she cries for help; the voice on the other end tells her that this is an "SOS line for victims of violence." The next shot shows her lying in a shelter bed crying. There she meets another woman, Zhana, and they share their horrific stories—one visual and the other oral. The information provided by the two women is compared and complemented through a series of cross-cut flashbacks.

After a "loverboy," Kosta, seduces the main unnamed heroine, he drives her to a motel where she is left in the hands of a pimp. The only rape scene occurs in the motel and is filmed with a handheld camera situated beside the two bodies, the man on top of his victim. The camera shakes in close proximity to the fully clothed bodies, and it is difficult for the viewer to recognize any particular body parts; the camera rapidly moves from left to right with the rhythm of the rape to convey the violated woman's pain rather than expose her body. After a few more jerky movements, the spectator's gaze is directed to her motionless, crying face (Plate 44). The film, even more than *Lady Zee*, focuses on the emotional and mental trauma of the female characters, rather than on their physical abuse.

Director Maria Tsitseva chose to center on the emotional devastation of the two women, as the whole (forty-minute) film depicts the painful and slow process that the characters are going through, trying to understand what happened to them and why. Since *You Are Alive* was commissioned and used by Open Gate in their prevention campaign, it is understandable that the focus is on the survival of trafficked women and the process of recovery. In the film, both women begin to recognize their trauma by re-telling and remembering their horrific experiences, a first step in the recovery process, while living in the shelter.

Svetlana's Journey is the only example here that represents a US/ Bulgaria co-production (Journey Film Group of filmmaker Micheal Cory Davis and Bulgarian Topform). It portrays the violation and sexual abuse of a teenage girl, Svetlana, who after her mother's death is betrayed by her relatives and sold to pimps. The betrayal and the sale are presented in the first few scenes, while the rest of the cinematic narrative focuses on Svetlana's shock and trauma at the hands of her pimps. The film opens with a sketchy and unclear scene in which Svetlana is taken to a dark dilapidated apartment. There, a young woman delivers her to a dreadful looking couple, who, after a degrading examination of her body and some dissatisfaction with her weight, pay to acquire her. This is the first shocking scene, as well as the first one to suggest the disturbing reality of trafficked women. The rest of the film continues to exploit distressing scenes of Svetlana's abuse, then, after forty odd minutes, ends with her suicide.

In *Svetlana's Journey*, the body-examining episode, especially its lighting (dark interior and soft light focused only on Svetlana's face) and décor (1970s furniture and wallpaper that have lost their color), set the tone for Svetlana's experience of abuse and suffering. Viewers are invited to identify with Svetlana's cruel objectification at the hands of the pimps. A close-up focuses briefly on the pimp's angry face, then jumps and stays more attentively on Svetlana's while the pimp's cruel fingers are examining her skin and opening her mouth to check her teeth (Plate 45).

The handheld camera and the close proximity to her face create an uneasy, even sickening effect early on in the film. These episodes determine the rest of the narrative, which relies entirely on shocking images and provides very little other information that can build a more comprehensive and perhaps more credible or accurate presentation of trafficking. If the first scene of Svetlana's sale invites identification with her pain and can evoke either, as Kaplan and Wang suggest, "the position of being vicariously traumatized" or "the position of being a witness," the next scene, of Svetlana's abuse, borders on overindulgence. A handheld camera follows the beating and drowning of Svetlana in the bathroom. Blood, aggression, and the girl's loud screaming create an intense and disturbing impression. The director, however, decided to spend considerable cinematic time on it, which can most likely shock the viewer and turn him or her away.

In the role of Svetlana, Violeta Markovska's acting is natural and "organic" (to use Stanislavsky's term), and the camera work (attentive close-ups or jittery moves) convincingly express the young girl's pain and trauma. Svetlana's voice-over, writing and reading from her diary, pushes the film's sense to that of the documentary and has the potential to work as what Hesford calls "testimony"—although in this case, Svetlana's first person narration does not recount her trauma but her bewilderment, confusion, and fear. Testimony can work as a rhetorical marker in an effort to evoke empathy and create the witnessing spectator. Although Svetlana's diary functions as an escape mechanism for her, for the viewer the diary scenes reinforce the character's helplessness and innocence, thus evoking emotional empathy. Overall, *Svetlana's Journey* reveals ambiguous techniques that can either move the viewer with Svetlana's sad story, or the (excessive and lengthy) images of violence against her can risk shocking the viewer, thus turning him or her away from the problem.

These East European cinematic examples of traumatic trafficking visuals together with the last co-production show that there is a fragile line between seeking to create an empathetic viewer and titillating the spectator with the objectification of female bodies. Although, more than their Western counterparts, they attempt to sympathize with trafficked characters, I do not in any way claim that this divide can be generalized or that this conclusion of a more sensitive depiction of women's violation in the Bulgarian and Macedonian films is valid for all East European trafficking films. On the contrary, these examples, paired with the ambiguity of the effect of *Svetlana's Journey*, only demonstrate that across national and regional cinemas, the balance between achieving empathy or voyeurism is very delicate.

There are, however, other elements of the film narratives, combined with the viewer's cultural and gender identities, that contribute to the effectiveness of these traumatic scenes. Traumatic images per se do not create engaged citizens. As Hirsch and Kaplan argue, the "context" and "background information" of the traumatic images, as well as the spectator's "conceptual horizons," are as important as the traumatic images. All of these elements of the cinematic narrative and the extra-cinematic concept about the "conceptual horizon" of the spectator relate to the question: How do these traumatic trafficking scenes influence different audiences?

The Trafficking Film and the (Dis)Believing Spectator

To the "banality of evil," which can describe some people's persistent indifference to the problem of trafficking, artists, communities, and governments have timidly responded with the "fragility of goodness"— a response evident in all films and NGO materials discussed in the book, among other legal and social actions. *Fragility of Goodness* is the title of Tzvetan Todorov's book, which describes Bulgaria's efforts and actions to save its Jews during World War II, evocatively referencing Arendt's "banality of evil," with which she described Adolf Eichmann's participation in the Holocaust. By reporting on his trial for *The New Yorker*, she concluded that he showed neither guilt nor hatred, and this "indifference" characterized the conditions enabling the Holocaust. Todorov studied the events and the involvement of various Bulgarian groups (parliamentarians, lawyers, the Church, and ordinary people) that prevented the deportation of the Bulgarian Jews (from Bulgaria proper, not the occupied territories) during World War II and con-cludes that unforeseen developments accompanying the goodwill of everyone concerned made the campaign successful.

The media's interest in trafficking is commendable, but I have opted for Todorov's phrase precisely because I see not only the good-ness, but also its fragility. No doubt, the increased media and govern-mental involvement deserves praise, but it also begs a more critical analysis. The representation of violence and abuse requires particular attention and understanding, for it hides latent conflicts between evoking catharsis and inciting titillation.[3]

---

[3] Torchin's chapter "Traffic Jam: Film, Activism, and Human Trafficking" offers useful information on how films and media on trafficking have been used by NGOs and policy makers, but does not elaborate on how and if they reach regular viewers (Torchin 2010, 218–237).

"Goodness" (or social activism) stems from our desire for meaning, or, more precisely, for meaningful social engagement, which, however, is inseparable from the desire for pleasure rooted in sexuality and the body. Thus, "goodness" commands both the sublimity of culture and its social activism on the one hand, and the brutality of acting out on the other. The tension or conflict between the social engagement of culture and its propensity to act out creates conditions for the fragile existence of "goodness." This double bind attraction to the virtual representations of trafficking and the trauma it engenders implicates both filmmakers and viewers. In his book *Representing the Holocaust*, LaCapra exposes the risk—which Caruth's approach to trauma hides—of ignoring the possibilities of social involvement and change:

> In my discussion, I have suggested a linkage in recent theory of acting-out not only with possession by the repressed past, repetition compulsions, and unworked- through transference but also with certain models of performativity, inconsolable melancholy, and the sublime [...]. The discovery of Paul de Man's World War II journalism or the revival of the question of Heidegger and the Nazis functioned in certain quarters as a kind of return of the repressed. But at times reactions have involved the reiteration of modes of reading and interpretation that abet the tendency to trope away from specificity and to reprocess problems in terms of reading technologies that function as discursive "cuisinarts." Such reactions inhibit processes of working-through and learning from the past. (LaCapra, 1996, 209–10)

In November 2006, the Animus Association Foundation in Sofia organized a film festival on trafficking films, which were screened (free of charge) in a well-known Sofia cinema-theater (Plate 46). The films included *Human Trafficking, Lady Zee, Last Resort* (director Pawel Pawlokowski UK, 2000), *Lilya 4-ever, Promised Land, Maria Full of Grace* (director Joshua Marston US/Colombia, 2004), and *Svetlana's Journey*. After each screening, the viewers received a questionnaire, which included two basic questions: 1) Did you learn something new about trafficking in people from this film? What?; and 2) Did you believe the story of the film? Why? I do not have a statistical analysis of the data and offer only a qualitative interpretation of the results. 107 responses were received. A considerable majority of spectators answered the two questions positively. Interestingly, twenty-five people indicated that they had learned nothing new about trafficking from these films, and only five people expressed disbelief in the story. In other words, about 77 percent learned something new and 95 percent found the films credible. An immediate conclusion comes to mind, namely that these Bulgarian viewers are much less perceptive and critical than film scholars or critics. Another possible explanation of the results concerns the context of the screening as part of a festival dedicated to trafficking prevention that offered films for educational purposes, free of charge. The information (or the content) mattered more than the form. Viewers predominantly responded to the second question with "Yes, because a story like that can happen in life. (Da, zashtoto podobni sluchai ima.)" They were obviously indifferent to the way the story was delivered, with one notable exception.

All five negative answers to the second question and six of the negative responses to the first question come from viewers of one particular film, *Svetlana's Journey*. Fourteen viewers in total responded to this film. Apparently, a higher percentage (78 percent) of viewers left the screening of *Svetlana's Journey* having learned nothing or doubting, compared to viewers who were content with the credibility of other films they watched. Negative answers include statements such as "Most things were not real and they do not correspond to Bulgarian reality. (Povecheto neshta ne biaha realni i ne otgovariat na bulgarskata deistvitelnost);" "It appears as an isolated case, not typical for human trafficking. (Izglezhda e chasten sluchai, koito ne e tipichen za trafikiraneto na hora.);" and "The theme was not defended professionally. (Temata ne e zashtitena profesionalno.)"

It is important to reiterate that *Svetlana's Journey* is an American-Bulgarian co-production of American writer/director Davis and a Bulgarian NGO, Face-to-Face. The other Bulgarian film, *Lady Zee*, had better success: thirty-two people responded, with eight (25 percent) noting that they did not learn anything new about trafficking from it, and all thirty-two believing the story. All other films (foreign productions to the Bulgarian audience) achieved a similar level of effectiveness, with 18 percent of viewers (on average) learning little new about trafficking but all believing the story. Watching these films more critically, one can easily argue, as already shown, that some present better cinematic narratives, acting, and camera work than others. Yet the fact that Bulgarian viewers appear to be more perceptive (or critical) of films that directly reflect their own reality (or films, in which the context of the trafficking experience is culturally familiar), obviously plays an important role in the way these films deliver their messages.

Prompted by these results, I screened *Svetlana's Journey* to seventy American students in an Introduction to Bulgarian Culture course, and asked them the same two questions. All answers to both questions were positive. Representative answers comprised of: "I learned how horrible trafficking can be;" "Yes, that even women take part in it; "Yes, I believe it was credible because the movie had such a realistic tone;" and "I felt, it could be pretty accurate." These responses obviously contradict the Bulgarian reactions which found the story inaccurate, especially in terms of its representation of Bulgarian reality. The American positive outcome is also backed by the praise the film received in the United States when screened at festivals. It took the award for BEST SHORT SUBJECT at The Hollywood Film Festival and Best HD Short and Runner Up for Best Director at the HD Film Festival (both 2005).

It is necessary to remind the reader briefly of the study that explored the cross-cultural differences on the level of knowledge and attitudes towards the problem of trafficking in people, discussed in Chapter 3. These differences affect not only viewers but filmmakers as well. Before turning my attention to the creators' conceptual horizons, I explicate how the films can contribute to building better informational horizons for the viewer, as the study clearly identified that the level of information is important for the overall eagerness to take action against trafficking. Although this study did not examine the accuracy of information about trafficking students profess to have, it is important to be equipped with facts and not myths.

Returning to the negative responses of Bulgarian viewers to *Svetlana's Journey*, I acknowledge that five answers are not statistically significant, but when they are considered against the background of the fourteen viewers of the film and the 107 surveyed viewers of all the films, these five disbelieving responses, along with their answers mentioned above, ought to be seen as a sign of dissatisfaction with the film. To add to this, my seventy American students expressed no doubts.

The overall picture of the responses begs the question about the cultural horizon of the viewers and the way *Svetlana's Journey* relates to it. While the traumatic images of Svetlana's violation in *Svetlana's Journey* have shown the potential to evoke empathy in the spectator, there are other aspects of this film that poke holes in the credibility of the overall presentation. Each of the characters, especially the pimps, Ivan (Maksim Genchev) and Violeta (Gergana Dzhikelova), are not three-dimensional, but flat. The dialogue in Bulgarian is unnatural and full of clichés. This stereotypical dialogue contributes to the forceful and artificial acting of Genchev and Dzhikelova. And last but not least, the narrative leaves the spectator confused about numerous inconsistencies: 1) What is the relationship between Ivan and Violeta? 2) Why do they live in such unthinkable conditions (the state of the apartment is repulsive), if Svetlana makes 400 euros daily and they collect the money? and 3) What kind of electrician (a client of the pimps) can afford to pay Svetlana's rates (if she makes 400) and who (if paying 50 euros) will frequent such a locale?[4] Moreover, even though poverty and unemployment characterize the Bulgarian economy, the image of a homeless person warming himself by the fire, the decrepit apartment, and the dirty and rundown bathroom can certainly distance the spectator (especially Bulgarians) with the sensational insistence on desolation and melancholy. While Svetlana's performance and the traumatic images might evoke empathy, these discrepancies create suspicion and disbelief and negate the credibility of the story. I have no data on the public's reception of *Face Down*, but considering the Bulgarian viewers' dissatisfaction with *Svetlana's Journey*, I will not be surprised if the film is received with suspicion, too.

Unlike the Bulgarian viewers' negative response to the film and its critical analysis revealing flaws, US audiences and my Ohio State students viewed and accepted the stereotypical presentation of Bulgarian reality without question. Due to this uncritical reception by Westerners, it has been frequently used in trafficking prevention campaigns. On March 30, 2006, at an anti-trafficking reception in Sofia the US ambassador to Bulgaria, John Beyrle, remarked:

---

[4] Electricians in Bulgaria usually charge 10 euros for one or two hours of work.

The film, *Svetlana's Journey*, was shown on Nova Televizia (New Television) last December and has become an important weapon in the fight against human trafficking. It reminds me of the way that the American novel *Uncle Tom's Cabin* became a powerful symbol in the fight against slavery in the United States in the 19th century—it personalizes the tragedy of trafficking, and demands justice.[5]

The discrepancy between this (Western) praise of the film and the Bulgarian viewers' dissatisfaction with it, paired with the imperfections that this analysis brings to light, reveals the dicey nature of media involvement with trafficking. It is precisely these exaggerated and inaccurate cultural aspects of the cinematic narratives that contribute to the spectator's suspicion and disbelief in trafficking.

Western viewers, on the other hand, watching a stereotypical and exoticized construction of a land of trafficking, might adopt witnessing and empathic positions, moved by the powerful presentation of bodily violations, but they are also misled by the clichéd representations of the Bulgarian cultural context. Another question emerges here: How helpful are these films in expanding the information horizon of Western viewers if they offer somewhat deceptive information about trafficking and the conditions that define it? All the Western films discussed in Chapter 4 reveal the same objectification and exoticization of East European realities and people. In my classroom, none of my American students detected any misconstruction of Bulgarian culture. To them, the film offered enough information about trafficking and they all believed the story. According to their responses, this film achieved its goal to raise awareness.

Contrary to the presentation of the cultural context in *Svetlana's Journey*, *Lady Zee* depicts the realities of Bulgarian orphans, petty criminals, and people with social and economic disadvantages with sensitivity and understanding. The scenes in the orphanage and at the home of Zlatina's mother, a Christian Roma, whom Zlatina meets for the first time, reveal an interior of necessities, clean and neatly arranged. Even the useless toys donated to the orphanage and piled up in the

---

[5] I was present at the reception and quote here from memory.

corner communicate the authenticity of the atmosphere. It is interesting to note that most actors in the film are amateurs, young girls and boys from Bulgarian orphanages, and only Naiden, the athlete (Ivan Burnev), is a professional actor. Nobody appears as a caricature of a criminal or pimp, as Ivan does in *Svetlana's Journey*. The scenes at the shooting range frequented by criminals are depicted without any temptation for exaggeration. The criminals wear their typical sweat suits naturally and comfortably, unlike Ivan, who is portrayed topless with a thick gold chain and gold teeth. Stereotypical and cartoonish images of criminals underestimate the intelligence of the audience.

The tragic heroine, Zlatina, a Roma woman who would like to be perceived as Bulgarian and rejects her Roma mother, is played movingly by Vanina Chervenkova. She is a tough tomboy and a marksman; therefore her decision to use her femininity to achieve freedom is heartbreaking—this decision crushes all her strength and willpower. *Lady Zee* received numerous film festival awards (Sofia, Montreal, Belgrade, Trieste) and participated in many international festivals, mostly in Eastern Europe but also in Spain, Denmark, and Germany. The film became one of the best-received films in Bulgaria.

Another example can be added to Western/East European co-productions like *Svetlana's Journey*. An adventure story, *Bucharest Express* (2002), unfolds in an imaginary Southeastern European country, Bekova, where a young female journalist investigates stories of trafficked girls and stumbles upon an international ring of criminal organizations connected to Bekova's corrupt officials. According to the film's website, "*Bucharest Express*, a film by Chuck Portz, is a feature-length motion picture produced by SawHorse Productions from the US and Moldova-Film Studio."[6]

Containing no images of bodily abuse and violation, the film opts instead for a repetitive narration of trafficking cases by relatives of women affected by trafficking or by the main protagonists themselves, who regale one another with their personal stories. Vera, the journalist, is aided by her British friend Jack, his local wife Svetlana, and an American journalist, Michael—a coupling that immediately exposes

---

[6] Chuck Portz has produced, written, and/or directed three films for PBS, for which he received a Writers Guild nomination for best screenplay (Bucharest Express).

the stereotypical gender construct, positioning the Western men in a dominant relationship with East European women.

One can argue that the verbal repetition of the trafficking cases, together with Vera's testimonial voice-over describing her difficulties in investigating trafficking cases, invites viewers to adopt the witnessing (or empathic) position, but the very construction of the adventure plot and the participation of its agents destabilize the credibility of the story. No perceptible conflict drives the story, which merely depicts laughably inept criminals who fail to capture or kill the characters seeking the truth. The four major characters themselves are presented as good-hearted amateurs who enjoy one another's company, develop romantic relationships, and manage to expose an international net of criminal organizations and corrupt local officials. Moreover, the filmmakers exoticize the local culture by including a colorful and completely implausible scene with Roma musicians, invited to entertain the characters at one of their enjoyable gatherings, a picnic in the countryside. Like *Svetlana's Journey*, the film has been well received in the United States, mainly at church event screenings or university campuses, and has been awarded numerous prizes.

Just to remind the reader, the Macedonian film *You Are Alive* is much more faithful to local realities, as it respectfully presents the conditions of a shelter for violated women. As mentioned in Chapter 2, I did not discover evidence of disbelief in the story that the film presents. Only some viewers were surprised that trafficking happens in Macedonia. The film was shown mainly in Macedonia, but also in Berlin at the Balkan Black Box Festival (November 2005).

To avoid Kaplan's "empty empathy," knowledge and cultural awareness are essential. Even if the positions promoted by Kaplan and Wang are vestigially present in the viewers' perceptions of *Svetlana's Journey* and *Bucharest Express*, they do reflect the cultural insensitivity of the film's creators, who speak *for* affected subjects, not *with* them. Despite the directors' good intentions, they produce culturally suspicious and implausible stories with psychologically weak characters, creating not the witnessing but the disbelieving spectator. Inaccurate cultural details, flawed narratives, and shallow characters in turn prompt viewers' suspicions.

While to the Western viewer these films most likely appear truthful and moving, they feed and perpetuate the stereotypical perception that the viewer may have of these countries. I contend that the films' effectiveness in the fight against trafficking is doubtful, since the informational horizons they present to Western audiences are fraught with misconceptions. These informational flaws in turn create an incomplete presentation of trafficking, since often such presentation does not implicate all elements of the problem. The "goodness" is fragile after all, as Todorov argues.

The Creator(s) and Good Intentions

Nobody doubts the good intentions of the American filmmakers of *Svetlana's Journey* and *Bucharest Express*, but the intentions do not always guarantee productive final results. Davis's website reports: "In 2003, while shooting two feature length films in Sofia, Bulgaria, Michael learned of the growing number of young girls and women forcefully taken from Bulgaria and other Balkan countries and exploited as prostitutes. Devastated by the story of a thirteen-year-old Bulgarian girl's abduction, Michael was inspired to write and direct *Svetlana's Journey*" (Davis 2016).

The statement testifying to Davis's accidental involvement and efforts that produced the film undoubtedly demonstrate what LaCapra calls working-through; that is, a possibility of argumentative justice that is self-questioning and related to action. Working-through is removed here from its therapeutic framework and allied to ethical and political considerations. Davis and the local teams of actors, cameramen, and technicians took action, created *Svetlana's Journey*—screened in Bulgaria and at international festivals—and thus opened a space for discussion and reflection on the problems of trafficking. At the same time, there are important aspects of the film—namely, its aesthetic weakness to deconstruct myths and clichés—that hinder the above intentions.

The engagement of the American director of *Bucharest Express* is not much different. The official website of the film states: "Chuck Portz has produced, written and/or directed three films for PBS: *Staus, My Man Bovanne* and *a Mistaken Charity*, for which he received a Writers Guild nomination for best screenplay. During his most recent trip to Moldova he completed research supported by a Fulbright grant.

For two years after its release the film was screened on college and university campuses (including Harvard, Yale, and Columbia), as well as church gatherings and local film festivals."

No one doubts that the creators of *Human Trafficking* were also socially motivated; for at least five years after the film aired on the Lifetime channel, it maintained an informative website presenting facts and figures about the phenomenon of trafficking. The film's main stars, Sutherland and Sorvino, gave interviews and participated in many anti-trafficking events. These goodwill activities, however, do not substantially correct the objectification of women that the film presents, nor do they improve the overall credibility of the film.

In contrast, Diulgerov, the Bulgarian director of *Lady Zee*, has not been publicly engaged with the topic of trafficking and his intentions and attempts at activism cannot be identified. While his film exposes a possible scenario of trafficking, it is not the very focus of the cinematic narrative. Rather, the director tells the story of an orphan, whose life ends tragically as a result of prostitution and trafficking. Critics point out that *Lady Zee* is a culmination of Diulgerov's artistic and ethical development (Dimitrova 2005). The subject of the destiny of Bulgarian orphans is morally charged and reveals the director's sensitivity to contemporary social issues. Unsurprisingly, viewers' comments on blogs relate mainly to the subject matter and not to the film's artistic power, although there are remarks about that as well.[7]

The question that emerges then is: Do filmmakers who are socially motivated always achieve their goal to raise awareness about trafficking and inspire viewers to take a stand? It is important to note here that *Svetlana's Journey* has been widely used by NGOs and the US government to promote prevention, whereas *Lady Zee* escaped the attention of social activists and policy makers but received many international awards. The answer to this question is naturally multifaceted.

As I have argued, there are various cinematic and extra-cinematic elements that contribute to an effective and influential trafficking film. I have investigated the power of traumatic images of rape and bodily violation, and contend that there is an elusive balance between titil-

---

[7] See http://forum.rozali.com/viewtopic.php?p=375803 [last accessed: September 10, 2016].

lating the viewer and provoking his or her social indignation. More importantly, I insist that disturbing visuals can shock East European viewers and propel them to learn more or become engaged with the fight against trafficking only if these images are well situated in accurate information of Eastern European realities or the trafficking phenomenon itself. Broadcasting precise and truthful information about trafficking without subjecting it to certain ideological views can only add to the power of traumatic images.

Some of the complexities of the cinematic engagement with trafficking are explored in *Moving People, Moving Images*. The introduction, for example, argues that: "the representation of trafficking poses significant challenges to those 'outside' (i.e. the non-trafficked/non-trafficking) observers who make films on the matter. Since it is an illicit practice, the networks and processes of trafficking are difficult to monitor" (Brown et al. 2010, 8). This difficulty persists, but NGOs and governments related to the problem have done a lot more work since *Moving People, Moving Images* was published.

Further in the book, Brown raises the question, "Can there be a film made by a person trafficked into Europe, or *must* trafficked people be represented by the Europeans that are complicit in their fates?" (2010, 43). While I explore the tension between national and international productions on trafficking, there have also been documentaries created with the active participation of survivors, such as *Open Your Eyes*, in which survivors tell their stories, mentioned in Chapters 2 and 3. Although trafficking survivors speak for themselves, the film reveals other narrative flaws, as analyzed by Hesford. Contrary to Brown's argument, Hesford effectively contends that the oppressed individual is not the only one capable of authentically delivering her story. She writes: "The assumption that the subject can speak only for herself, [is] a stance that ignores how rhetorical conventions and discursive systems shape the construction of subjectivity and agency" (2004, 107–108). To me, the question lies beyond Brown's theoretical axis, but within the sensitivity of the filmmakers to speak *with* the victims and not *for* them, with the compassion to respectfully and authentically present the cultural context of the story rather than to exaggerate circumstances in an attempt to stress the deplorable conditions, as well as in the understanding of viewers and their cultural and informational background.

Problems of cinematic representations of trafficking demand rephrasing and alternative approaches. As discussed in Chapter 4, most Western filmmakers are defined by a dominant ideology, which unconsciously affects their benevolent aims to get involved with the problems of trafficking and to raise awareness. Although one can argue that a creator can transcend dominant ideology through narrative structure, editing, and photography, the overall analysis of Western trafficking productions reveals a certain level of complacency with the worldview of capitalist hegemony. Here one is reminded of Dyer's argument that the problem is not in the construction of stereotypes per se but in people and their ideology that control this construction.

Doubting the ability of media and film to literally transmit trauma, Meek concludes: "In contrast to the 'transmission model' I argue in favor of an understanding of historical trauma in which the construction of specific events as traumatic is understood with reference to the politics of technological media and nation states, including their colonial ideologies and global impact" (2010, 195). Although I do not fully share Meek's skepticism, I am concerned with the effectiveness of Western media to raise awareness and create an action-oriented citizen. As my analysis reveals, while some films are more effective than others, the value of the shocking trauma that films offer is marred by other cinematic and extra-cinematic elements that affect the final products.

Afterword

The first part of this book focuses on national, cultural, and gender differences that in various ways determine people's general perception and understanding of trafficking. Social science studies and my work with NGOs in the Balkans reveal tensions between the global flow of trafficking information and images and their local comprehension. Various ideological factors, such as persistent views of center and periphery (us versus them) and the consequential power relations in economic and cultural exchanges, clearly mark both the perception and creation of trafficking films and media. Understanding this tension and the resulting attitudes and cultural products is vital for the ultimate goal of anti-trafficking campaigns to raise awareness and accurately educate people about this modern-day slavery. This tension also underlies the crucial question that film-creators, activists, and NGOs ought to ask: what kind of films to create and use. Screening trafficking is no doubt a prudent and perilous act, for it is fraught with ideological perspectives and implications, center-periphery power relations, gender inequalities, and the difficulties of generating well-informed and engaged viewers. Although I acknowledge that film creation results from various considerations, mostly genre norms and profitability, when the subject of the films is trafficking, they are often assumed to serve the purpose of educating citizens.

In this book, I describe, analyze, and categorize Western and East European feature films and media materials, as I point out certain narrative and cinematic flaws triggered by various economic, cultural, and production reasons. I investigate the accuracy with which they depict trafficking as well as their artistic qualities. My analysis pays attention to the genre and market aspects of Western anti-trafficking films and how they shape the final product alongside their (latent) ideological structure that presents a binary global world—a division which privileges the West. Western productions construct a black-and-white picture of the trafficking process, identifying criminals and victims as Eastern European and rescuers as Western, and ineffectively inform policymakers who often prefer to focus on the criminalization and international security side of trafficking while ignoring the economic imbalances in the world, the human rights aspects, and the Western negative impact as the demand region.

The analysis of South Eastern European films reveals that they depict trafficking actors (perpetrators, victims/survivors, and rescuers) differently. The Balkan productions show preoccupation with the moral and economic failure of their own communities and portray much more multifaceted trafficking situations, exposing local conditions that should inform government agencies and policymakers who ought to address the economic and social realities (including education) of target communities and their people's vulnerability to being trafficked. Undoubtedly, these films are not all equally effective in their attempts, but the filmmakers exhibit concerns that differ from those of their Western counterparts.

It is warranted here to address the depressing portrayal of East European communities in both Western and South Eastern films, a portrayal that at first might appear the same. I cannot stress enough that this first impression is clearly misleading, for the cultural background and the ideological motivation of the Balkan and Western filmmakers is different—a difference that underlies their approach to (South) East European realities and the impressions their films create. While Western films gaze, objectify and exoticize East European life and people, South Eastern European films reveal deep anxieties about the state of their own communities. Even though I have argued that an authentic representation of experience can be created not only by artists who have shared that experience, i.e. not only by insiders or, in these cases, East European filmmakers, but also by outsiders, Western filmmakers who are able to speak *with* rather than *for* communities affected by trafficking, most of the Western film-creators miss this rhetorical opportunity and speak *for* the trafficked persons and their societies.

In addition to the Western feature films which are generally ineffective for educating citizens and informing policymakers, Western anti-trafficking documentaries and media involvement with the problem have flaws ranging from inaccuracies and unjustified optimism to moral beliefs that blend trafficking and prostitution, as my discussion exposes. PBS, CNN, and Al Jazeera documentaries reveal ideologies that frame the trafficking stories. Their overall structures of interlinking survivors' testimonies with experts' interviews rely more on the subjectivity, experience, and opinions of both people affected by trafficking and those who attempt to combat it rather than on objective presentations based on research and data.

In her study of Slovenian media coverage in the early months of 2004, Pajnik also points out problems of "one-sidedness, vagueness, simplification, stereotyping" in the reports on trafficking; and Andrijašević's investigation of IOM/LaStrada counter-trafficking campaign posters in The Czech Republic, Ukraine and Moldova in the late 1990s and early 2000s identifies stereotypical depiction of East European women as "unhappy, desperate, and suicidal" (2007, 42). In contrast, some more recent NGO efforts discussed here suggest a new and more complex approach. Prevention campaigns materials of ASTRA, Open Gate, and Animus indicate an attempt to refocus the attention of audiences from sex trafficking to all forms of trafficking that target men and children, not only women. Cautiously, I contend that these materials shift public and government efforts from old ineffective tendencies discouraging people from seeking opportunities to better educating them and empowering them.

I aim to uncover other aspects of the films, namely the use of violence and shocking images, which can move viewers and make them witnesses to the traumatic trafficking experience. Being a witness, Kaplan and Wang argue, is the most valuable position that the viewer can assume, for s/he can become socially involved with the problem (2009). My analysis of the traumatic images and the way they are cinematically presented suggests that not all films effectively employ such images, as some tend to objectify women's bodies and create voyeurs. Finding Kaplan and Wang's theory about the spectator's possible positions vis-à-vis cinematic trauma constructive, I also study the cultural background of these images that the films provide as building the informational horizons of viewers. While East European viewers can be offended by inaccurate and exaggerated representations of their national and cultural realities, and therefore can underestimate the magnitude of the problem, Western audiences might miss these inaccuracies or accept them as fact. The films might not contribute to the expansion of their perspectives and knowledge of Eastern Europe, but they do help to evoke sympathy and hopefully activism. The problem these films present to Western viewers is the perpetuation of stereotypes about the (Eastern) other.

Completing the circle of investigation (beginning with the discussion of the viewer, his or her cultural conditions and attitudes towards trafficking, and moving to the analysis of various narrative and extra-narrative aspects of anti-trafficking films and media), the last chapter returns to the studies of cross-cultural differences among viewers and how these differences affect one's eagerness to take a stand against this twenty-first-century form of slavery. One can hope that truthful and authentic information leads to more effective involvement with the problem. My overall arguments show that representations of trafficking reach the spectator in a very complex manner, and the more we know about the ways audiences react to these films, the more educated and selective our approach to anti-trafficking materials should be.

To this complexity one can add yet another concern about the overall involvement of media and today's social media, especially Facebook Live and Twitter, with traumatic events and their consequences. Much was written in the aftermath of 9/11 about the media's contribution to peoples' reactions to and attitudes toward the disaster. Scholars like Sontag, Žižek, Kaplan, and Jacques Derrida elaborate on the very nature of media and its usefulness in such circumstances. *Two major opinions formed* as part of a heated debate in the letters section of *The London Review of Books* (Kaplan 2005, 16). While some intellectuals (mostly Europeans) viewed the event as a result of US international politics leading to hatred, Americans wanted to comprehend the attack in specific terms as a series of events. Close to the European voices, Sontag described the event as "a monstrous dose of reality" and the public reactions as "self-righteous drivel being peddled by public figures and TV commentators" (2001, 23). In an interview, Derrida spoke of the event and the intense media attention as an attempt to "conjure away" the anxieties that it provoked and the inability to comprehend its significance (Borradori 2003, 87). In turn, Žižek's article "Welcome to the Desert of the Real!" insists that the reality outside the United States, constructed by the long history of colonialism and imperialism, "returned" as a traumatic memory after the occurrence of 9/11 (2003, 133). He even argues that Americans perhaps unconsciously anticipated the event in many films with similar catastrophes. While Kaplan appreciates Žižek's argument about the unconscious "anticipation" of the attack, she disagrees with his broad generalizations and abstractions:

> But this [Žižek's] thesis does not at all exhaust or actually get close to the specificity of the event for those of us living close by. It is possible that the Towers represented to the terrorists (perhaps schooled in American movies) postmodernity, technology, the city, architectural brilliance, urban landscape, the future high-tech, globalized world. But for those nearby, they functioned phenomenologically as part of people's spatial universe, in and of themselves, not especially representing American capitalism or American might. (2005, 15–16)

One can certainly object to Kaplan's view that the Towers did not necessarily represent the American might because on a certain level of existence in the United States, all people are subject to the ideology of supremacy, regardless of the conscious attempts of many to resist and challenge such an ideology. But I offer these diverse sets of opinions here only to show the lack of agreement and consensus. In addition, these varied opinions indicate that the involvement of people and scholars with virtual trauma is a complex process and a delicate balance between "working through" and "acting out"—a balance that demands careful examination. As Kaplan argues against Žižek's generalizations, I reject the stereotypes and clichés evident in films and media on trafficking. The anti-trafficking feature films and media coverage, along with the prevention campaign materials of NGOs, similarly demand a delicate balance, as well as an accurate and objective presentation of perpetrators, survivors/victims, rescuers, and their societies—a presentation that does not create binary worlds, does not objectify women, and does not titillate the viewer, but creates a well-informed and engaged citizen. The prudent and perilous sides of screening trafficking warrant sincere and unbiased engagement with the problem, as well as a well-researched and critical selection of films and media.

Bibliography

Adorno, Theodor. 1991. *The Culture Industry: Selected Essays on Mass Culture.* London: Routledge.

Andrijašević, Rutvica. 2007. "Beautiful Dead Bodies: Gender, Migration and Representation in Anti-Trafficking Campaigns." *Feminist Review* 86: 24–44.

Animus Association. Animusassociation.org [last accessed: September 17, 2016].

Appadurai, Arjun. 1996. *Modernity at Large: Cultural Dimensions of Globalization.* Minneapolis: University of Minnesota Press.

ASTRA. http://www.astra.rs/about-astra/?lang=en [last accessed: August 2016].

Baker, Carrie. 2013. "Moving Beyond 'Slaves, Sinners, and Saviors': An Intersectional Feminist Analysis of US Sex-Trafficking Discourses, Law, and Policy." *Journal of Feminist Scholarship* 4: 1–23. http://www.jfsonline.org/issue4/articles/baker/ [last accessed: September 17, 2016].

Bakhtin, Mikhail. 1990. "Author and Hero in Aesthetic Activity." In *Art and Answerability: Early Philosophical Essays,* edited by M. Holquist and V. Liapunov, 4–256. Austin: University of Texas Press.

Bales, Kevin and Ron Soodalter. 2009. *The Slave Next Door.* Berkeley: University of California Press.

Barnett, Antony and Solomon Hughes. 2001. "British firm accused in UN 'sex scandal.'" *The Guardian* July 28. https://www.theguardian.com/world/2001/jul/29/unitednations [last accessed: September 17, 2016].

Berman, Jacqueline. 2004. "Media Constructions and Migration Projects: Trafficking in Women in an International Migration (Management) Frame." In *Women and Trafficking,* edited by Simona Zavratnik Zimic, 41–63. Ljubljana: Peace Institute.

Bernstein, Elizabeth. 2007. "The Sexual Politics of the 'New Abolitionism'." *Differences: a Journal of Feminist Cultural Studies* 18(3): 128–51.

Borradori, Giovanna. 2003. *Philosophy in a Time of Terror: Dialogues with Jurgen Habermas and Jacques Derrida.* Chicago: University of Chicago Press.

Bozhinova, R., Tair, E. 2005. "Personality characteristics and interpretation of negative mass media presentation." *Proceedings of the 3rd National Congress of Psychology*, Sofia, 28–30 October 2005, edited by Djonev et al. SOFI-R Press, 24–28 (in Bulgarian).

———. 2008. "Media violence – short-term and long-term effects". *Psychological Investigation* 1: 33–49 (in Bulgarian).

———. 2009. "Youth's perceptions about the reality in Bulgaria." *Psychological Investigation* 3: 30–45 (in Bulgarian).

Bozhinova, Rumiana, Yana Hashamova, and Ergyul Tair. 2010. "Knowledge and Attitudes Towards Trafficking in People: Cross-Cultural Differences." *Bulgarian Journal of Psychology* 1(4): 41–51.

Brown, William, Dina Iordanova, and Leshu Torchin. 2010. *Moving People, Moving Images: Cinema and Trafficking in the New Europe.* St. Andrews, Scotland: St. Andrews Film Studies (College Gate Press).

Brown, William. 2010. "Negotiating the Invisible." In *Moving People, Moving Images: Cinema and Trafficking in the New Europe*, by William Brown, Dina Iordanova, and Leshu Torchin, 16–49. St. Andrews: College Gate Press.

Byars, Jackie and Eileen Meehan. 1994. "Once in a Lifetime: Constructing 'The Working Woman' through Cable Narrowcasting." *Camera Obscura* 33–34: 13–41.

Caruth, Cathy. 1996. *Unclaimed Experience: Trauma, Narrative and History.* Baltimore: John Hopkins University Press.

Chatterjee, Choi and Beth Holmgren. 2013. Introduction to *Americans Experience Russia: Encountering the Enigma, 1917 to the Present*, edited by Choi Chatterjee and Beth Holmgren, 1–11. London: Routledge.

Comisso, Ellen and Brad Gutierrez. 2004. "Eastern Europe or Central Europe? Exploring a Distinct Regional Identity." In *The Politics of Knowledge: Area Studies and the Disciplines*, edited by David Szanton, 263–314. Berkeley: University of California Press.

Covering Media. 2011. "The Whistleblower." http://www.coveringmedia. com/movie/2011/08/the-whistleblower.html [last accessed: September 17, 2016].

Davies, John. 2009. *'My Name Is Not Natasha': How Albanian Women in France Use Trafficking to Overcome Social Exclusion (1998–2001).* Amsterdam: Amsterdam University Press.

Davis, Michael Cory. 2016. "Biography." Michael Cory Davis. http://michael-corydavis.com/biography/ [last accessed: September 17, 2016].

Deans, Jason. 2004. "Sex Traffic Drives Viewers to Channel4." *The Guardian* October 15. https://www.theguardian.com/media/2004/oct/15/overnights [last accessed: September 17, 2016].

Deltcheva, Roumiana. 2005. "Reliving the Past in Recent East European Cinemas." *East European Cinemas*, edited by Aniko Imre, 197–211. London: Routledge.

Dimitrova, Genoveva. 2005. "Leidi Zi (Lady Zee)." *Kultura*. http://www.kultura.bg/ media/my_html/2392/kino.htm [last accessed: September 17, 2016].

Dinan, Kinsey Alden. 2008. "Globalization and national sovereignty: From Migration to Trafficking." In *Trafficking in Human$: Social, Cultural and Political Dimensions*, edited by Sally Cameron and Edward Newman, 58–79. Tokyo: United Nations University Press.

Doane, May Ann. 1990. "Remembering Women: Psychical and Historical Constructions in Film Theory." In *Psychoanalysis and Cinema*, edited by E. Ann Kaplan, 46–64. London: Routledge.

Doezema, Jo. 1999. "Loose Women or Lost Women? The re-emergence of the myth of 'white slavery' in contemporary discourses of 'trafficking in women'." http://www.wal net.org/csis/papers/ doezema-loose.html [last accessed: June 3, 2016].

Dyer, Richard. 2002. *The Matter of Images: Essays on Representations*. 2nd edition. London: Routledge.

————. 2004. "The Role of Stereotypes." *In Media Studies: A Reader*, edited by Paul Marris and Sue Thornham, 245–52. New York: New York University Press.

Ebert, Roger. 2009. "Taken." *Chicago Sun-Times*, Janury 29. http://rogerebert.suntimes.com/apps/pbcs.dll/article?AID=/20090128/REVIEWS/901289987/1023 [last accessed: October 8, 2016].

————. 2007. "Eastern Promises." http://www.rogerebert.com/reviews/eastern-promises-2007 [last accessed: October 8, 2016].

Ekov, E. 2009. "10,000 Bulgarian are victims of trafficking in people." Newspaper *Monitor* April 29 (in Bulgarian).

Elliott, Mark. 2005. "Christian responses to trafficking in women from Eastern Europe." *East-West Church & Ministry Report* 13(3): 1–6.

European Commission, 2009. http://ec.europa.eu/bulgaria/press_corner/news/250309-children_bg.htm [last accessed: October 8, 2016].

European Union Agency for Fundamental Rights (FRA). 2015. *Severe labour exploitation: workers moving within or into the European Union: States' obligations and victims rights*. Luxembourg: Publications Office of the European Union.

ERRC. "Macedonia: a Report by the European Roma Rights Centre: Country Profile 2011-2012." http://www.errc.org/cms/upload/file/macedonia-country-profile-2011-2012.pdf [last accessed: October 8, 2016].

Felman, Shoshana and Dori Laub, M.D. 1992. *Testimony: Crisis of Witnessing in Literature, Psychoanalysis and History.* New York: Routledge.

Fiske, John. 1989. "Moments of Television: Neither the text nor the Audience." In *Remote Control: Televisions, Audiences and Cultural Power,* edited by E. Seiter, H. Borchers, G. Kreutzner and E.M. Worth, 56–78. London: Routledge.

———. 2003. *The John Fiske Collection: Television Culture.* 2nd edition. London: Routledge.

Fleming, Mike Jr. 2011. "Sex Trafficking feature 'Whistleblower' Gets UN Screening Tomorrow." *Deadline/Hollywood* October 13. http://www.deadline.com/2011/10/sex-trafficking-feature-the-whistleblower-gets-un-screening-tomorrow/ [last accessed: October 8, 2016].

Geertz, Clifford. 1973. *The Interpretation of Cultures: Selected Essays.* New York: Basic Books.

Ghodsee, Kristen. 2010. *Muslim Lives in Eastern Europe: Gender, Ethnicity, and the Transformation of Islam in Postsocialist Bulgaria.* Princeton: Princeton University Press.

Goscilo, Helena and Margaret B. Goscilo. 2014. *Fade from Red: The Cold War Ex-Enemy in Russian and American Film 1990–2005.* Washington, DC: New Academia Publishing.

Gotovski, Mikhail. 2010. "Monitoring na sludski predmeti od oblasta na trgovijata so luge i ilegalnata migratsija vo Makenodija 2010 godina." http://all4fairtrials.org.mk/wp-content/uploads/2016/06/Izvestaj_2011_MKD.pdf [last accessed: October 8, 2016].

Gramsci, Antonio. 1998. *Prison Notebooks: Selections.* London: Lawrence and Wishart.

Guerin, Frances and Roger Hallas. 2007. *The Image and the Witness: Trauma, Memory, and Visual Culture.* London: Wallflower Press.

Hajdinjak, Marko. 2002. "Smuggling in Southeast Europe: the Yugoslav Wars and the Development of Criminal Networks in the Balkans" CSD Paper No. 10, Center for the Study of Democracy. http://unpan1.un.org/intradoc/groups/public/documents/UNTC/UNPAN016836.pdf [last accessed: October 8, 2016].

Halloran, James. 1970. "The Social Effects of Television." In *The Effects of Television,* edited by James Halloran, 24–68. London: Panther Books.

Hashamova, Yana. 2007. *Pride and Panic: Russian Imagination of the West in Post-Soviet Film.* Bristol, UK: Intellect Ltd.

———. 2015. "Looking for the Balkan (Br)other: Representations of Bulgarians in Russian Film." *The Russian Review* 74 (April): 211–29.

Hesford, Wendy. 2004. "Documenting Violations: Rhetorical Witnessing and the Spectacle of Distant Suffering." *Biography* 27(1): 104–44.

———. 2005. "*Kairos* and the Geoplotical Rhetorics of Global Sex Work and Video Advocacy." In *Just Advocacy?: Women's Human Rights, Transnational Feminisms, and the Politics of Representation*, edited by Wendy Hesford and Wendy Kozol, 146–73. New Brunswick: Rutgers University Press.

Hirsch, Joshua. 2009. "Post-traumatic Cinema and the Holocaust Documentary." In *Trauma and Cinema: Cross-Cultural Explorations*, edited by E. Ann Kaplan and Ban Wang, 93–123. Aberdeen: Hong Kong University Press.

Hopkins, R. and Nijboer, J. 2004. "Trafficking in human beings and human rights: Research, policy and practice in the Dutch approach." In *Human Rights Law Review* Special Issue Spring: 75–90.

Hutchings, Stephen. 2008. *Russia and its Other(s) on Film: Screening Intercultural Dialogue*. Houdmills: Plagrave Macmillan.

Imre, Anikó (ed). 2005. *East European Cinemas*. London: Routledge.

Iordanova, Dina. 2003. *Cinema of the Other Europe: The Industry and Artistry of East Central European Film*. New York: Wallflower Press.

——— (ed). 2006. *The Cinema of the Balkans*. London: Wallflower Press.

IWPR. 2003. "Trading in Misery." Institute for War and Peace Reporting September 15. http://www.iwpr.net/?p=bcr&s=f&o=156034&apc_state=henibcr2003 [last accessed: October 8, 2016].

Johnston, Claire. 1985. "Women's Cinema as Counter Cinema." In *Movies and Methods* Vol. 2, edited by Bill Nichols, 208–23. Los Angeles: University of California Press.

Johnson, Ericka. 2007. *Dreaming of a Mail-Order Husband*. Durham: Duke University Press.

Kaes, Anton. 2009. *Shell Shock Cinema: Weimar Culture and the Wounds of War*. Princeton: Princeton University Press.

Kang, Liu. 1998. "Is There an Alternative to (Capitalist) Globalization?: The Debate about Modernity in China." In *The Cultures of Globalization*, edited by Fredric Jameson and Masao Miyoshi, 164–90. Durham: Duke University Press.

Kaplan, E. Ann. 1990. "Introduction: From Plato's Cave to Freud's Screen." In *Psychoanalysis and Cinema*, edited by E. Ann Kaplan, 1–24. London: Routledge.

———. 1997. *Looking for the Other: Feminism, Film and the Imperial Gaze*. New York: Routledge.

———. 2005. *Trauma Culture: The Politics of Terror and Loss in Media and Literature*. New Brunswick: Rutgers University Press.

Kaplan, E. Ann and Ban Wang. 2009. "Introduction." In *Trauma and Cinema: Cross Cultural Explorations*, edited by E. Ann Kaplan and Ban Wang, 1–23. Aberdeen: Hong Kong University Press.

Kapur, Geeta. 1998. "Globalization and Culture: Navigating the Void." In *The Cultures of Globalization*, edited Fredric Jameson and Masao Miyoshi, 191–217. Durham: Duke University Press.

Kempadoo, Kemala. 2011. "Introduction." In *Trafficking and Prostitution Reconsidered: New Perspectives on Migration, Sex Work, and Human Rights* 2nd ed., edited by Kemala Kempadoo with Jyoti Saghera and Bandana Pattanaik, vii–xlii. London: Routledge.

Kennedy, Michael. 1994. "An Introduction to East European Ideology and Identity in Transformation." In *Envisioning Eastern Europe: Postcommunist Cultural Studies*, edited by Michael Kennedy, 1–45. Ann Arbor: University of Michigan Press.

Kesić, Obrad. 1999. "Women and Gender Imagery in Bosnia: Amazons, Sluts, Victims, Witches, and Wombs." In *Gender Politics in the Western Balkans: Women and Society in Yugoslavia and the Yugoslav Successor States*, edited by Sabrina P. Ramet, 187–202. University Park, PA: Pennsylvania State University Press.

Kesić, Vesna. 2000. "From Reverence to Rape: and Anthropology of Ethnic and Genderized Violence." In *Frontline Feminisms: Women, War, and Resistance*, edited by Marguerite R. Waller and Jennifer Rycenga, 23–36. New York: Garland Publishing.

Kit, Borys. 2010. "Rachel Weisz's 'The Whistleblower' Picked Up By Samuel Goldwyn Films." *The Hollywood Reporter* November 4. http://www.hollywoodreporter.com/blogs/risky-business/rachel-weiszs-whistleblower-picked-samuel-35825 [last accessed: October 8, 2016].

Kitzenger, Jenny. 1999. "A Sociology of Media Power: Key Issues in Audience Reception Research." In *Message Received*, edited by Greg Philo, 3–21. Harlow: Pearson.

Klapper, J. T. 1969. *The Effects of Mass Communication.* Glencoe: Free Press.

Kligman, Gail and Stephanie Limoncelli. 2005. "Trafficking Women after Socialism: To, Through, and from Eastern Europe." *Social Politics: International Studies in Gender, State and Society* 12(1): 118–40.

Kristensen, Lars Lyngsgaard Fjord. 2007. "Divergent Accounts of Equivalent Narratives: Russian–Swedish *Interdevochka* meets Swedish–Russian *Lilya 4-ever*." *Portal: Journal of Multidisciplinary International Studies* 4(2): 1–24.

Lacan, Jacques. 1981. *Four Fundamental Concepts of Psycho-Analysis*, translated by Alan Sheridan. New York: W.W. Norton & Company.

LaCapra, Dominick. 1996. *Representing the Holocaust: History, Theory, Trauma.* Ithaca, NY: Cornell University Press.

LaStrada. "Video zapisi." http://www.lastrada.org.mk/index.php/welcome_mk/videozapisi [last accessed: October 9, 2016].

Lehti, Martti. 2003. "Trafficking of Women and Children in Europe." HEUNI Paper No. 18, The European Institute for Crime Prevention and

Control. http://www.heuni.fi/uploads/to30c6cjxyah11.pdf [last accessed: October 9, 2016].

Limoncelli, Stephanie. 2010. *The Politics of Trafficking.* Stanford: Stanford University Press.

Lindstrom, Nicole. 2004. "Regional Sex Trafficking in the Balkans: Transnational Networks in an Enlarged Europe." *Problems of Post-Communism* 51(3): 45–52.

Longinović, Tomislav. 2005. "Playing the Western Eye: Balkan Masculinity and Post Yugoslav War Cinema." In *East European Cinemas*, edited by Anikó Imre, 35–49. London: Routledge.

Macdonald, Myra. 2009. "Politicizing the Personal." In *Media Studies: A Reader*, edited by Sue Thornham, Caroline Bassett, and Paul Marris, 656–70. New York: New York University Press.

Mateeva, Elitsa. 2015. "S litse nadolu. Spasenie niama." (Face Down. There is No Salvation). http://12mag.net/pop/s-litse-nadolu-spasenie-nyama/#sthash.0TLh435B.dpuf [last accessed: October 12, 2016].

Marx, Karl. 1886. *Capital.* New York: Humboldt.

Mayne, Judith. 1990. *The Woman at the Keyhole: Feminism and Women's Cinema.* Bloomington: Indiana University Press.

—. 1993. *Cinema and Spectatorship.* London: Routledge.

McQuail, Denis. 1969. *Towards a Sociology of Mass Communication.* London: Macmillan.

Meek, Allen. 2010. *Trauma and Media: Theories, Histories, and Images.* New York-London: Routledge.

Melegh, Attila. 2007. *On the East/West Slope: Globalization, Nationalism, Racism and Discourses on Eastern Europe.* Budapest-New York: Central European University Press.

Morley, David. 1980. *The 'Nationwide' Audience.* London: BFI.

Mulvey, Laura. 1989. "Visual Pleasure and Narrative Cinema." In *Visual and Other Pleasures* 14–26. Bloomington: Indiana University Press.

National Commission for Combating Traffic in Human Beings. http://antitraffic.government.bg/ [last accessed: October 12, 2016].

———. January 2008. "Sociological Study Public Opinion and Public Attitudes to Trafficking in Human Beings." http://antitraffic.government.bg/images/documents/Polezna_informacia/EN/Researches/1254918665.pdf [last accessed: October 12, 2016].

———. April 2008. "Sociological Study Trafficking in Human Beings—Connotations, Meanings, Attitude and Expectations of the Institutions." http://antitraffic.government.bg/images/documents/Polezna_informacia/EN/Researches/1254918474.pdf [last accessed: October 12, 2016].

————. 2009. "Sociological Study Trafficking in Human Beings Class." http://antitraffic.government.bg/images/documents/Polezna_informacia/EN/Researches/1254918341.pdf [last accessed: October 12, 2016].

Neumann, Iver. 1996. *Russia and the Idea of Europe.* London: Routledge.

————. 1999. *Uses of the Other: "The East" in European Identity Formation.* Minneapolis: University of Minnesota Press.

Norris, Stephen and Zara Torlone (eds.). 2008. *Insiders and Outsiders in Russian Cinema.* Bloomington: Indiana University Press.

Open Gate – La Strada Macedonia. http://www.lastrada.org.mk [last accessed: October 12, 2016].

Pajnik, Mojca. 2004. "Trafficked Women in Media Representations." In *Women and Trafficking,* edited by Simona Zavratnik Zimić, 63–73. Ljubljana: Mirovni Institut.

Papadimos, Sophia. 2012. "Human Trafficking in Serbia and Greece: a Comparative Analysis of a Victim-Centered Approach." M.A. Thesis, The Ohio State University.

Poncheva, Monika. 2015. "'S litse nadolu – za izkuplenieto i spasenieto" (Face down – about redemption and salvation). http://www.vesti.bg/analizi-i-komentari/komentari/s-lice-nadolu-za-izkuplenieto-i-spasenieto-6042728 [last accessed: October 12, 2016].

Pratt, Ray. 2001. *Projecting Paranoia: Conspiratorial Visions in American Film.* Lawrence: University Press of Kansas.

Prince, Stephen.1992. *Visions of Empire: Political Imagery in Contemporary American Film.* New York: Praeger.

Prvi i najveći ženski forum. 2011. http://www.ana.rs/forum/index.php?topic=140204.0 [last accessed: October 12, 2016].

Pulver, Andrew. 2010. "The Wizard behind the Camera." *Directors Guild of America* Spring. http://www.dga.org/Craft/DGAQ/All-Articles/1001-Spring-2010/Profile-David-Yates.aspx [last accessed: June 3, 2016].

Pumpitout. 2011. "Cynthia McKinney Grills Donald Rumsfeld." Rebroadcast of C-SPAN coverage. https://www.youtube.com/watch?v=yMG65jYlDU8 [last accessed: October 12, 2016].

Said, Edward. *Orientalism.* London: Vintage, 1979.

Schuckman-Matthews, Emily. 2015. "Potraying Trafficking in Lukas Moodysson *Lilya 4-ever.*" *Feminist Media Studies* 15(5). http://dx.doi.org/10.1080/14680777.2015.1009930 [last accessed: October 12, 2016].

Shales, Tom. 2005. "'Human Trafficking': Exploiting Misery, And Creating it." *The Washington Post* October 24. http://www.washingtonpost.com/wp-dyn/content/article/2005/10/23/AR2005102301514.html [last accessed: October 12, 2016].

Shaw, Tony and Denise Youngblood. 2010. *Cinematic Cold War: The American and Soviet Struggle for Hearts and Minds.* Lawrence, KS: University Press of Kansas.

Silver, Kristen. 2010. "Human Trafficking in the United States: Citizen Empathy & Awareness." Research Honor Thesis in Psychology, The Ohio State University. http://kb.osu.edu/dspace/handle/1811/58810 [last accessed: October 12, 2016].

Soderlund, Gretchen. 2005. "Running from the Rescuers: New US Crusades Against Sex Trafficking and the Rhetoric of Abolition." *National Women's Studies Association Journal* 17(3): 64–87.

Sontag, Susan. 1977. *On Photography.* New York: Straus and Giroux.

———. 2001. Editorial in "The Talk of the Town." *The New Yorker* September 24: 32.

Šošić, Anja. 2009. "Put lubenica." *Zapis.* http://www.hfs.hr/nakladnistvo_zapis_detail.aspx?sif_clanci=32558#.V1HZr-QyM9s [last accessed: July 7, 2016].

Stanley, Alessandra. 2005. "Selling Sex, That Renewable Resource." *The New York Times* October 24. http://www.nytimes.com/2005/10/24/arts/television/24traf.html?_r=2& [last accessed: October 12, 2016].

Stiglmayer, Alexandra, ed. 1994. *Mass Rape: The War against Women in Bosnia-Herzegovina,* translated by Marion Faber. Lincoln, NE: University of Nebraska Press.

Suchland, Jennifer. 2013. "Double Framing in *Lilya 4-Ever*: Sex Trafficking and Postsocialist Abjection." *Journal of European Cultural Studies* 16(3): 362–76.

———. 2015. *Economies of Violence: Transnational Feminism, Postcolonialism, and the Politics of Sex Trafficking.* Durham: Duke University Press.

Szabo, Amy. "A Global Problem with a Local Face: The Development of Human Trafficking for Sexual Exploitation in Serbia and Bosnia-Herzegovina." M.A. Thesis, The Ohio State University.

Todorov, Tzvetan. 2003. *The Fragility of Goodness: Why Bulgaria's Jews Survived the Holocaust,* translated by Arthur Denner. Princeton: Princeton University Press.

Todorova, Maria. 1994. "The Balkans: From Discovery to Invention," *Slavic Review* 53(2): 453–82.

———. 1997. *Imagining the Balkans.* Oxford: Oxford University Press.

Todorova, Sasha. 1999. "Emerging Poverty in Bulgaria." In *Poverty in Transition and Transition in Poverty,* edited by Yogesh Atal, 77–102. New York: Berhahn Books.

Torchin, Leshu. 2010. "Traffic Jam: Film, Activism and Human Trafficking." In *Moving People, Moving Images: Cinema and Trafficking in the New Europe,* by William Brown, Dina Iordanova, and Leshu Torchin, 218–37. St. Andrews: College Gate Press.

Toumarkine, Doris. 2007. "Eastern Promises." *Film Journal International.* http://www.filmjournal.com/filmjournal/esearch/article_display.jsp?vnu_content_id=1003637583 [last accessed: October 12, 2016].

UN.GIFT. *Films on Human Trafficking. February 2008.* United Nations Office on Drugs and Crime. Marcel van den Heuvel, Vienna, 2008.

———. "Films on Human Trafficking." http://www.ungift.org/knowledgehub/media/films.html [last accessed: October 12, 2016].

UN Panel Discussion of *The Whistleblower.* 2011. http://www.unmultimedia.org/tv/webcast/2011/10/panel-discussion-sexual-exploitation-and-abuse-in-conflict-and-post-conflict-situations.html [last accessed: October 12, 2016].

United Nations. 2000. "Protocol Against the Smuggling of Migrants by Land, Sea and Air, Supplementing the United Nations Convention Against Transnational Organized Crime." http://www.unodc.org/documents/southeastasiaandpacific/2011/04/som-indonesia/convention_smug_eng.pdf [last accessed: October 12, 2016].

———. 2002. Office of the Spokesman for the Secretary General. "Use of Sanctions Under Chapter VII of the UN Charter: the Former Yugoslavia," January. http://www.un.org/News/ossg/fy.htm [last accessed: October 12, 2016].

United States Department of State (USDOS). 2010. "Trafficking in Persons Report 2010." http://www.state.gov/j/tip/rls/tiprpt/2010/ [last accessed: October 12, 2016].

———. *Trafficking in Persons Report.* http://www.state.gov/documents/organization/226844.pdf [last accessed: October 12, 2016].

———. "Progress in Combating Trafficking in Persons: The Obama Administrations Accomplishments (as of February 2012)." http://www.state.gov/j/tip/rls/reports/pitf/185971.htm [last accessed: October 12, 2016].

Vance, Carole 2012. "Innocence and Experience: Melodramatic Narratives of Sex Trafficking and Their Consequences for Law and Policy." *History of the Present* 2(2): 200–18.

Vighi, Fabio. 2006. *Traumatic Encounters in Italian Film: Locating the Cinematic Unconscious.* Bristol, UK: Intellect.

Volkova, Elena. 1996. "Odinokii volk v poiskahk liubvi, very i Natashi." *Mir razvlechenii* (January 15): 26–27.

Wilson, T.D. 2000. "Human Information Behavior." *Special issue on Information Science Research* 3(2): 49–55.

Wolff, Larry. 1994. *Inventing Eastern Europe: The Map of Civilization on the Mind of the Enlightenment.* Palo Alto: Stanford University Press.

Wood, Robin. 1986. *Hollywood from Vietnam to Reagan.* New York: Columbia University Press.

Zhang, Sheldon. 2009. "Beyond the 'Natasha' story: a review and critique of current research on sex trafficking." *Global Crime* 10(3): 178–195.

Zimmerman, C., Hossain, M., Yun, K., Gajdadziev, V., Guzun, N., Tchomarova, M. et al. 2008. "The Health of Trafficked Women: a Survey of Women Entering Post trafficking Services in Europe." *American Journal of Public Health* 98 (1): 55–59.

Zimmerman C. & Watts C. 2007. "Documenting the effects of trafficking in women." In *Public Health and Human Rights: Evidence-Based Approaches,* edited by Beyrer, C., & Pizer, H., 143–77. Baltimore: Johns Hopkins University Press.

Žižek, Slavoj. 2000. *Ticklish Subject: The Absent Centre of Political Ontology.* London: Verso.

———. 2003. "Welcome to the Desert of the Real!" In *Dissent from the Homeland: Essays after September 11,* edited by Stanley Hauerwas and Frand Lentricchia, 131–35. Durham: Duke University Press.

Name Index

Subject Index

Film, Television, and Media Titles Index

TELEVISION PRODUCTIONS

FILMS and DOCUMENTARIES

SHORT FILMS